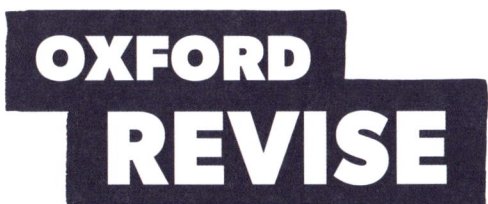

EDEXCEL GCSE

HISTORY

Superpower relations and the Cold War, 1941–91

COMPLETE REVISION AND PRACTICE

Series Editor: Aaron Wilkes

Richard McFahn
Kat O'Connor
Tim Williams

Contents

 Shade in each level of the circle as you feel more confident and ready for your exam.

How to use this book   iv

1 Early tension between East and West   2
- Knowledge
- Retrieval
- Practice

2 The development of the Cold War   8
- Knowledge
- Retrieval
- Practice

3 The Cold War intensifies   14
- Knowledge
- Retrieval
- Practice

4 Cold War crises: Berlin, 1958–61   20
- Knowledge
- Retrieval
- Practice

5 Cold War crises: Cuba   24
- Knowledge
- Retrieval
- Practice

6 Cold War crises: the Prague Spring   28
- Knowledge
- Retrieval
- Practice

7 Changing relationship between the superpowers   32
- Knowledge
- Retrieval
- Practice

8 The collapse of the USSR   38
- Knowledge
- Retrieval
- Practice

How to use this book

This book uses a three-step approach to revision: **Knowledge**, **Retrieval**, and **Practice**.
It is important that you do all three; they work together to make your revision effective.

 Knowledge

Knowledge comes first. Each chapter starts with a **Knowledge Organiser**. These are clear easy-to-understand, concise summaries of the content that you need to know for your exam. The information is organised to show how one idea flows into the next so you can learn how everything is tied together, rather than lots of disconnected facts.

Answers and Glossary

You can scan the QR code at any time to access sample answers, mark schemes for all the exam-style questions, a glossary containing definitions of the key terms, as well as further revision support go.oup.com/OR/GCSE/Ed/Hist/Superpower

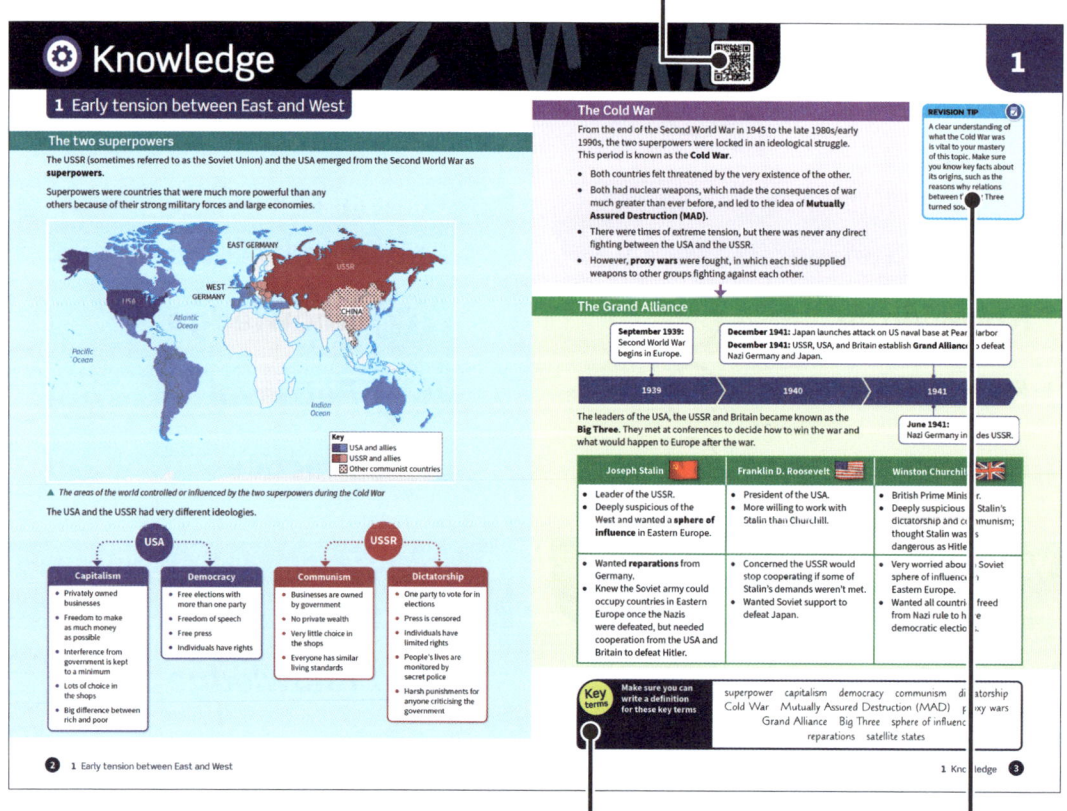

Key terms — Make sure you can write a definition for these key terms

The **Key terms** box highlights the key words and phrases that you need to know, remember and be able to use confidently.

REVISION TIP

Revision tips offer you helpful advice and guidance to aid your revision and help you to understand key concepts and remember them.

Retrieval

The **Retrieval questions** help you learn and quickly recall the information you've acquired. These are short questions and answers about the content in the Knowledge Organiser you have just reviewed. Cover up the answers with some paper and write down as many answers as you can from memory. Check back to the Knowledge Organiser for any you got wrong, then cover the answers and attempt all the questions again until you can answer *all* the questions correctly.

Make sure you revisit the Retrieval questions on different days to help them stick in your memory. You need to write down the answers each time, or say them out loud, otherwise it won't work.

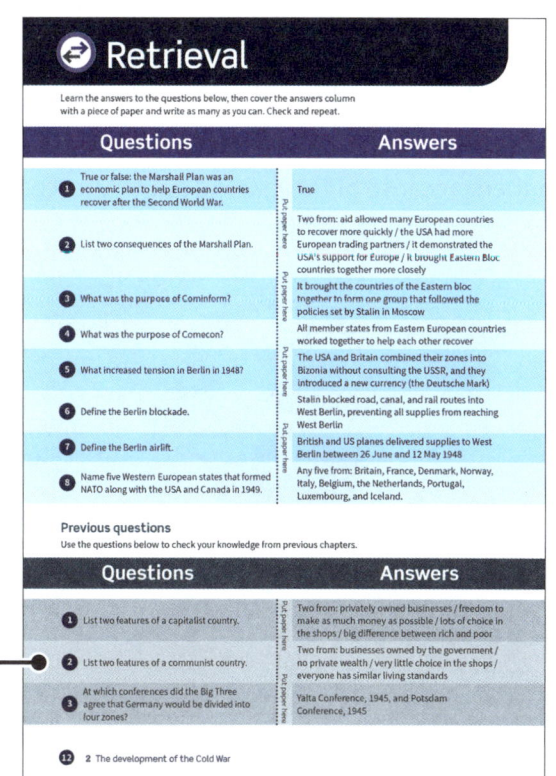

Previous questions

Each chapter also has some **Retrieval questions** from **previous chapters**. Answer these to see if you can remember the content from the earlier chapters. If you get the answers wrong, go back and do the Retrieval questions for the earlier chapters again.

Practice

Once you think you know the Knowledge Organiser and Retrieval answers really well, you can move on to the final stage: **Practice**.

Each chapter has **Exam-style Questions**, including some questions from previous chapters, to help you apply all the knowledge you have learnt and can retrieve.

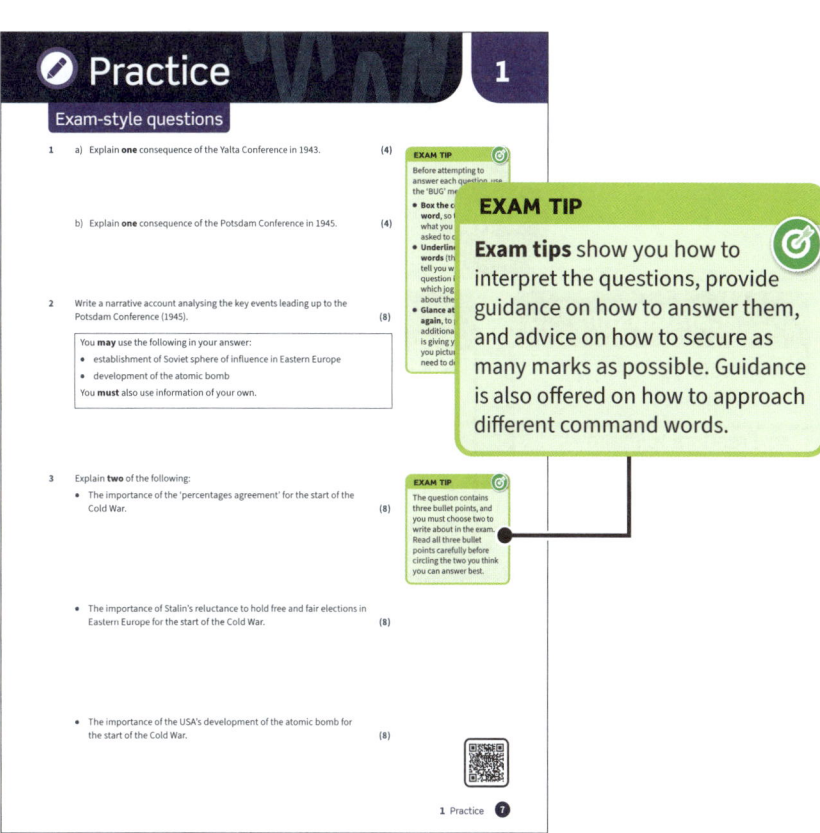

EXAM TIP

Exam tips show you how to interpret the questions, provide guidance on how to answer them, and advice on how to secure as many marks as possible. Guidance is also offered on how to approach different command words.

Knowledge

1 Early tension between East and West

The two superpowers

The USSR (sometimes referred to as the Soviet Union) and the USA emerged from the Second World War as **superpowers**.

Superpowers were countries that were much more powerful than any others because of their strong military forces and large economies.

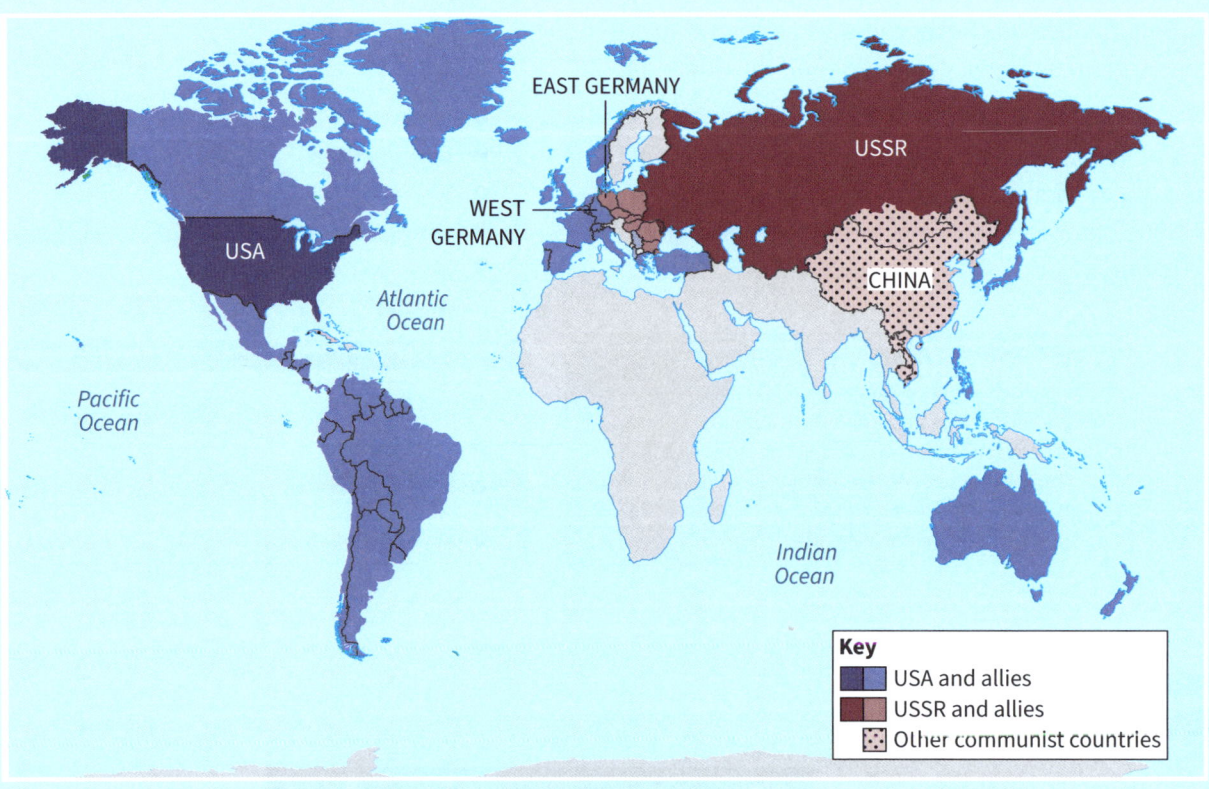

▲ The areas of the world controlled or influenced by the two superpowers during the Cold War

The USA and the USSR had very different ideologies.

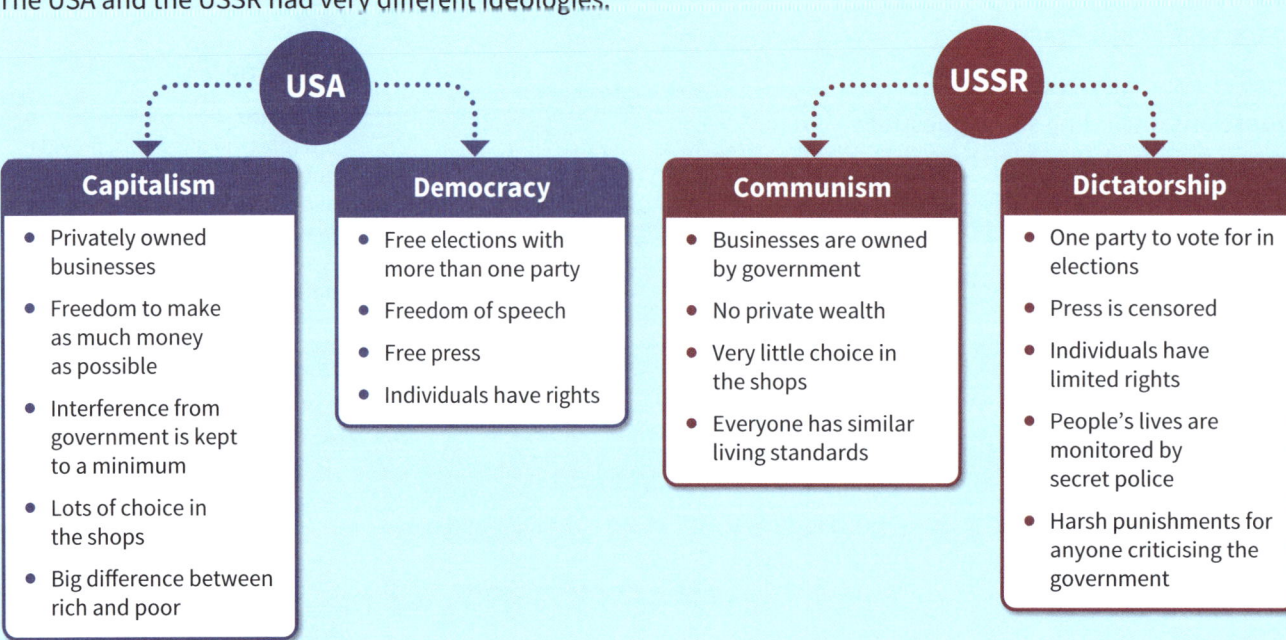

USA

Capitalism
- Privately owned businesses
- Freedom to make as much money as possible
- Interference from government is kept to a minimum
- Lots of choice in the shops
- Big difference between rich and poor

Democracy
- Free elections with more than one party
- Freedom of speech
- Free press
- Individuals have rights

USSR

Communism
- Businesses are owned by government
- No private wealth
- Very little choice in the shops
- Everyone has similar living standards

Dictatorship
- One party to vote for in elections
- Press is censored
- Individuals have limited rights
- People's lives are monitored by secret police
- Harsh punishments for anyone criticising the government

The Cold War

From the end of the Second World War in 1945 to the late 1980s/early 1990s, the two superpowers were locked in an ideological struggle. This period is known as the **Cold War**.

- Both countries felt threatened by the very existence of the other.
- Both had nuclear weapons, which made the consequences of war much greater than ever before, and led to the idea of **Mutually Assured Destruction (MAD)**.
- There were times of extreme tension, but there was never any direct fighting between the USA and the USSR.
- However, **proxy wars** were fought, in which each side supplied weapons to other groups fighting against each other.

> **REVISION TIP**
> A clear understanding of what the Cold War was is vital to your mastery of this topic. Make sure you know key facts about its origins, such as the reasons why relations between the Big Three turned sour.

The Grand Alliance

September 1939: Second World War begins in Europe.

December 1941: Japan launches attack on US naval base at Pearl Harbor.
December 1941: USSR, USA, and Britain establish **Grand Alliance** to defeat Nazi Germany and Japan.

1939 → 1940 → 1941

June 1941: Nazi Germany invades USSR.

The leaders of the USA, the USSR, and Britain became known as the **Big Three**. They met at conferences to decide how to win the war and what would happen to Europe after the war.

Joseph Stalin	Franklin D. Roosevelt	Winston Churchill
• Leader of the USSR. • Deeply suspicious of the West and wanted a **sphere of influence** in Eastern Europe.	• President of the USA. • More willing to work with Stalin than Churchill.	• British Prime Minister. • Deeply suspicious of Stalin's dictatorship and communism; thought Stalin was as dangerous as Hitler.
• Wanted **reparations** from Germany. • Knew the Soviet army could occupy countries in Eastern Europe once the Nazis were defeated, but needed cooperation from the USA and Britain to defeat Hitler.	• Concerned the USSR would stop cooperating if some of Stalin's demands weren't met. • Wanted Soviet support to defeat Japan.	• Very worried about a Soviet sphere of influence in Eastern Europe. • Wanted all countries freed from Nazi rule to have democratic elections.

Key terms — Make sure you can write a definition for these key terms

superpower   capitalism   democracy   communism   dictatorship
Cold War   Mutually Assured Destruction (MAD)   proxy wars
Grand Alliance   Big Three   sphere of influence
reparations   satellite states

Knowledge

1 Early tension between East and West

Tehran Conference, December 1943

Agreements made by the Big Three

- ✓ A plan to invade Nazi-occupied Europe was drawn up.
- ✓ The Soviets would join the USA's war against Japan once Hitler had been defeated.

In 1944, Churchill and Stalin met again and made the 'percentages agreement'. They agreed countries in Eastern Europe should be divided between the Soviets and the West when the war was won. Churchill would later regret this.

Yalta Conference, February 1945, with Nazi Germany on the brink of defeat

Agreements made by the Big Three

- ✓ Most countries in Eastern Europe would come under the Soviet sphere of influence.
- ✓ There should be free and fair elections in the countries liberated from Nazi occupation.
- ✓ Germany, and its capital city, Berlin, would be divided into four zones run by the USSR, USA, Britain, and France.
- ✓ The USSR could take reparations from Germany.
- ✓ The USSR would join the war against Japan.

Disagreements

- ✗ The USSR disagreed with the West over the type of government that would take control in Poland after the war.
- ✗ Stalin wanted to keep control of land in Poland and, although Poland's borders were discussed, they were not finalised.

Potsdam Conference, July and August 1945, after Nazi Germany has been defeated

Tensions at Potsdam:

- Following Yalta, Stalin established a Soviet sphere of influence in Eastern Europe. When the Red Army freed a country from Nazi rule, they helped set up a communist dictatorship. The USA and Britain were concerned that the free and fair elections agreed to at Yalta would never take place.
- New US president Harry Truman was much more anti-communist than Roosevelt.
- During the conference, Churchill was replaced as prime minister in Britain by Clement Atlee.
- The day before the conference began, the USA successfully tested the first ever atomic bomb. It gave the USA a significant military advantage over the USSR. It also meant that the USA would not need Soviet help to defeat Japan.
- With Hitler dead, Nazi Germany defeated, and Japan close to defeat, there was far less motivation for the USA and the USSR to work together. They no longer had a common enemy.

Agreements made

- ✓ The plan to divide Germany, and its capital city Berlin, into four zones run by the USSR, the USA, Britain, and France was finalised.
- ✓ Germany would pay reparations to the Allies, with most going to the USSR in the form of industrial equipment.

Disagreements

- ✗ Stalin, Truman, and Atlee disagreed about how harshly to punish Germany. Stalin wanted to damage Germany, but the West did not want to weaken it too severely.
- ✗ Stalin was reluctant to hold free elections in countries in Eastern Europe, in case communist parties loyal to him lost.

The atomic bomb

The use of atomic bombs against Japan in August 1945 ended the Second World War but it also increased tensions between the superpowers. Many historians argue it marked the beginning of the Cold War.

- Truman did not to tell his allies that the USA's new bomb was a nuclear bomb.
- Stalin's spies found out and it confirmed to him that the USA could not be trusted.
- It showed that the USA was determined to be the most powerful post-war country and was now a threat to the USSR.
- Stalin wanted the USSR to develop its own nuclear weapons.

The Long Telegram, February 1946

George Kennan, the second in command of the USA Embassy in Moscow, sent a telegram to the USA. In it, he said that he believed:

- the USSR was determined to spread its influence as far as possible
- the USSR was an enemy of the USA
- any attempt at cooperation with the USSR was doomed to failure.

The Novikov Telegram, September 1946

Nikolai Novikov, the Soviet Ambassador in the USA, sent a telegram to Moscow. In it, he said that he thought:

- the USA was determined to spread its influence as far as possible
- the USA was economically powerful
- the USA should not be trusted.

The Iron Curtain descends

Between 1945 and 1948, Stalin gradually ensured that enough people in the governments of the countries of Eastern Europe were communist and loyal to him. These countries became the USSR's **satellite states**; they seemed like independent countries but were dominated by the USSR.

The creation of the Eastern bloc, shown in orange in the diagram, was a key reason for the start of the Cold War. By 1946, the USA had committed itself to stopping the spread of communism.

▶ A map of Eastern Europe showing the satellite states of the USSR

Retrieval

Learn the answers to the questions below, then cover the answers column with a piece of paper and write as many as you can. Check and repeat.

Questions | Answers

#	Question	Answer
1	Define the term 'superpower'.	A country that is much more powerful than any others because of its military force and large economy
2	List two features of a capitalist country.	Two from: privately owned businesses / freedom to make as much money as possible / interference from government is kept to a minimum / lots of choice in the shops / big difference between rich and poor
3	List two features of a communist country.	Two from: businesses owned by government / no private wealth / very little choice in the shops / everyone has similar living standards
4	List three things Stalin wanted when he joined the Grand Alliance in 1941.	A sphere of influence in Eastern Europe, reparations from Germany, cooperation from the USA and Britain to defeat Hitler
5	What did Roosevelt want when he joined the Grand Alliance in 1941?	Soviet support to defeat Japan
6	What did Churchill want when he joined the Grand Alliance in 1941?	All countries freed from Nazi rule to have democratic elections
7	What was the 'percentages agreement'?	Agreement between Churchill and Stalin after the Tehran Conference in December 1943 about how countries in Eastern Europe should be divided between the Soviets and the West after the war
8	At which conference did the USSR, the USA, and Britain agree that there should be free and fair elections in the countries liberated from Nazi occupation?	Yalta Conference in 1945
9	At which conferences did the Big Three agree that Germany would be divided into four zones?	Yalta Conference, 1945, and Potsdam Conference, 1945
10	List three reasons why there were tensions at the Potsdam Conference in 1945.	Three from: the USSR had established a sphere of influence in Eastern Europe / Truman, the new US president, was more anti-communist than Roosevelt / the USA had developed a nuclear bomb / they no longer had a common enemy
11	What two events are considered as important reasons for the start of the Cold War?	The USA's development of the atomic bomb; the establishment of the Eastern Bloc
12	List the three elements of the Long Telegram.	In it, George Kennan said: he believed the USSR was determined to spread its influence as far as possible / the USSR was an enemy of the USA / any attempt at cooperation with the USSR was doomed to failure

1 Early tension between East and West

Practice 1

Exam-style questions

1 **a)** Explain **one** consequence of the Yalta Conference in 1943. (4)

b) Explain **one** consequence of the Potsdam Conference in 1945. (4)

EXAM TIP

Before attempting to answer each question, use the 'BUG' method:
- **Box the command word**, so that you know what you are being asked to do.
- **Underline the key words** (the words that tell you which topic the question is about, and which jog your memory about the topic).
- **Glance at the question again**, to pick up any additional information it is giving you and to help you picture what you need to do.

2 Write a narrative account analysing the key events leading up to the Potsdam Conference (1945). (8)

> You **may** use the following in your answer:
> - establishment of Soviet sphere of influence in Eastern Europe
> - development of the atomic bomb
>
> You **must** also use information of your own.

3 Explain **two** of the following:
- The importance of the 'percentages agreement' for the start of the Cold War. (8)

EXAM TIP

The question contains three bullet points, and you must choose two to write about in the exam. Read all three bullet points carefully before circling the two you think you can answer best.

- The importance of Stalin's reluctance to hold free and fair elections in Eastern Europe for the start of the Cold War. (8)

- The importance of the USA's development of the atomic bomb for the start of the Cold War. (8)

1 Practice 7

Knowledge

2 The development of the Cold War

The Truman Doctrine

Communism was attractive to some European countries at the end of the Second World War, because it seemed like an effective way to build a fairer society after the devastation of war.

US President Harry Truman gave a speech to Congress in March 1947. Truman hated communism, and he sent a clear message to the Soviets that communist expansion in Europe had to end.

Truman stated:
- communism posed a real threat to the whole world, and the USA would work to stop communism from spreading
- the USA would support any country under the threat of becoming communist
- communism had to be 'contained' (kept where it was, in the countries where it already existed).

This policy of **containment** became known as the **Truman Doctrine**.

> The free peoples of the world look to us for support in maintaining their freedoms.
>
> If we falter in our leadership, we may endanger the peace of the world — and we shall surely endanger the welfare of our own nation.

▲ Harry Truman

The Marshall Plan

The Truman Doctrine established the United States' political policy towards communism. In 1947, the US government launched the European Recovery Plan – known as the **Marshall Plan** – to provide countries with the economic support they needed to rebuild after the war.

Aims
- To enable a quick economic recovery in Europe, making communism less attractive.
- To encourage European countries to work together, and to work with the USA.
- To create a market for American goods and help the US economy.

The Plan
- $13 billion US dollars was given to countries in Europe that **denounced** communism, accepted aid, and spent part of it on US goods.
- Aid was offered to all countries in Europe. 15 countries accepted aid, including the UK, France, Italy, West Germany, Greece, Turkey, Sweden, Norway, and Iceland. All Eastern European countries controlled by the USSR refused this aid.

Consequences
- Aid from the Marshall Plan allowed many European countries to recover much more quickly than they would have done alone.
- The American economy benefitted, as the USA had more European trading partners.
- It showed that the USA was committed to supporting Europe for the long term.
- Communism was prevented from spreading to Western Europe.
- The division between East and West Europe grew, with the East being influenced by the Soviets and the West by the USA.

Stalin's response to the Truman Doctrine and the Marshall Plan

Stalin believed the Truman Doctrine and the Marshall Plan were a threat to the communist countries in Eastern Europe and responded with Cominform and Comecon.

> **REVISION TIP**
>
> It is possible that organisations, ideas, and schemes such as the Truman Doctrine, the Marshall Plan, Cominform, and Comecon might appear in different types of exam questions. Make sure you know what they are, their importance, and how they are connected.

Cominform (established 1947)

1. Stalin saw the Truman Doctrine as a major threat to communism.
2. Stalin created the Communist Information Bureau, known as **Cominform**.
3. Cominform brought the countries of the Eastern bloc together to form one group that followed the policies set by Stalin in Moscow.

Comecon (established 1949)

1. Stalin saw the Marshall Plan as an example of **dollar imperialism** by the USA (the USA using its wealth to secure and spread capitalism around the world).
2. Stalin made it clear that Eastern European countries should not accept Marshall Aid.
3. Stalin created the Council for Mutual Economic Assistance, known as **Comecon**, as an alternative to Marshall Aid.
4. Countries who signed up for Comecon agreed to work together and share resources to rebuild their countries as equal partners. However, Comecon was tightly controlled in Moscow.

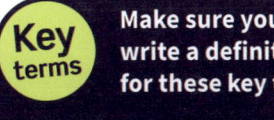 **Key terms** — Make sure you can write a definition for these key terms:

containment   Truman Doctrine   Marshall Plan   denounced   Cominform   Comecon   dollar imperialism   Bizonia   Berlin Blockade   Berlin Airlift   Federal Republic of Germany (FDR)   German Democratic Republic (GDR)   NATO   Warsaw Pact

Knowledge

2 The development of the Cold War

The causes of the Berlin Crisis (blockade and airlift)

- It was agreed at the Yalta conference and confirmed at the Potsdam conference in 1945 that Germany and its capital Berlin would be divided into four zones. The zones controlled by the USA, Britain, and France came to be known as West Germany, and the zone controlled by the USSR came to be known as East Germany.
- Berlin lay deep in Soviet-controlled East Germany.
- Using money from the Marshall Plan, the Western allies rebuilt their zones and heavily invested in their zones in Berlin.
- Stalin did not invest in his zone. Instead, the Soviets took German industrial equipment back to the USSR.

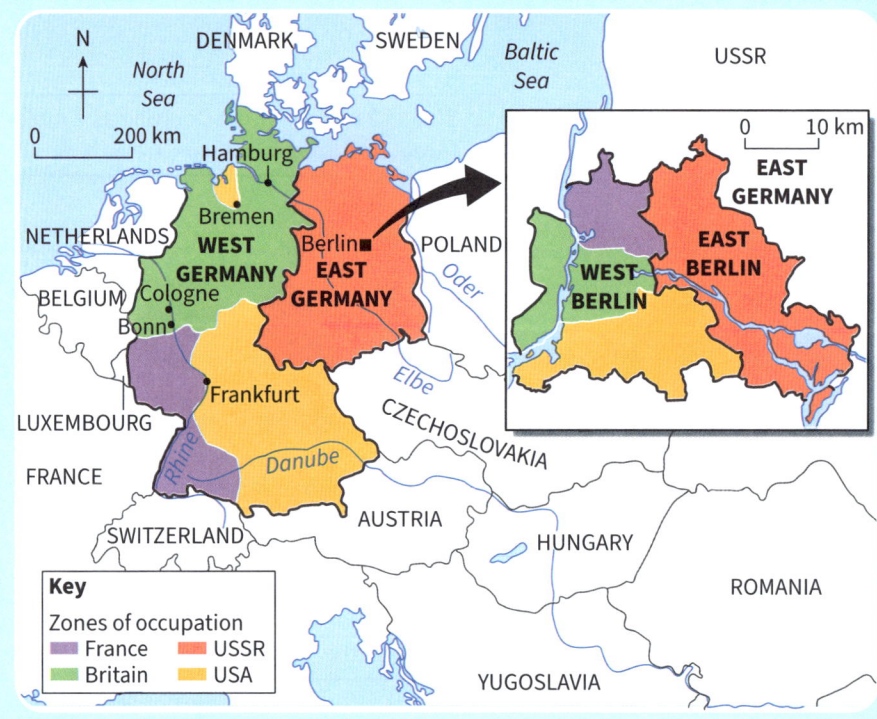

▲ The division of Germany as agreed at the Yalta and Potsdam Conferences in 1945.

- Standards of living increased in West Berlin and fell in East Berlin. This made capitalism look successful and communism unsuccessful. Stalin worried how this would affect people living in the Soviet zone in Berlin.
- Tension increased in March 1948 when the USA and Britain combined their zones into **Bizonia** (without consulting the USSR as previously agreed). Tensions increased further when they introduced a new currency, the Deutsche Mark, in June 1948. Stalin's fears of a strong capitalist West Germany grew.

Berlin Blockade

- Stalin wanted the Americans, British, and French to withdraw from Berlin and decided to make life difficult for them.
- Supplies reached West Berlin through Soviet-controlled East Germany and, on 24 June 1948, the Soviets began the **Berlin Blockade**.
- The Soviets blocked road, canal, and rail routes from West Germany to West Berlin, preventing food, fuel, and medical supplies from reaching West Berlin.
- This increased tension between the USA and the USSR: 2.5 million inhabitants of West Berlin had only six weeks of food and fuel left.

Berlin Airlift

- President Truman and Prime Minister Atlee wanted to avoid war with the USSR but did not want to abandon West Berlin.
- On 26 June 1948 British and US planes began delivering supplies to West Berlin.
- By the end of the airlift, over 2 million tonnes of supplies had reached West Berlin.
- On 12 May, Stalin finally backed down and ended the blockade. He realised it had failed; the West was not going to abandon West Berlin.

Consequences of the Berlin Blockade and Airlift

- The Berlin Blockade and Airlift had increased tension between the USA and USSR, and Berlin remained a hot spot throughout the Cold War.
- Stalin's fears were realised in May 1949 when the USA, France, and Britain formally merged their zones to create the **Federal Republic of Germany (FDR)**.
- Stalin retaliated in October 1949 by creating the **German Democratic Republic (GDR)**, a Soviet-style dictatorship.
- Western fear of Soviet aggression led to the formation of **NATO** in 1949.

The establishment of NATO and the Warsaw Pact

NATO

What? North Atlantic Treaty Organisation

When? Established April 1949

Why? In response to the Berlin blockade, Western European countries formed a defensive alliance, backed by the USA.

Membership? Twelve original members: USA, Canada, Britain, France, Denmark, Norway, Italy, Belgium, the Netherlands, Portugal, Luxemburg, and Iceland. Turkey and Greece joined in 1952. West Germany joined in 1955.

Weapons? As well as armies, NATO countries held nuclear weapons (USA from 1945, Britain from 1952, and France from 1960).

Warsaw Pact

What? An alliance created by the USSR in response to the creation of NATO.

When? Established May 1955

Why? The USSR and its satellite states became suspicious of NATO when West Germany joined in 1955. US troops were stationed in West Germany, so they formed a military alliance.

Membership? Eight members: USSR, Poland, East Germany, Czechoslovakia, Hungary, Romania, Bulgaria, and Albania.

Weapons? A combined army with over 5 million personnel, and the Soviet Union had nuclear weapons.

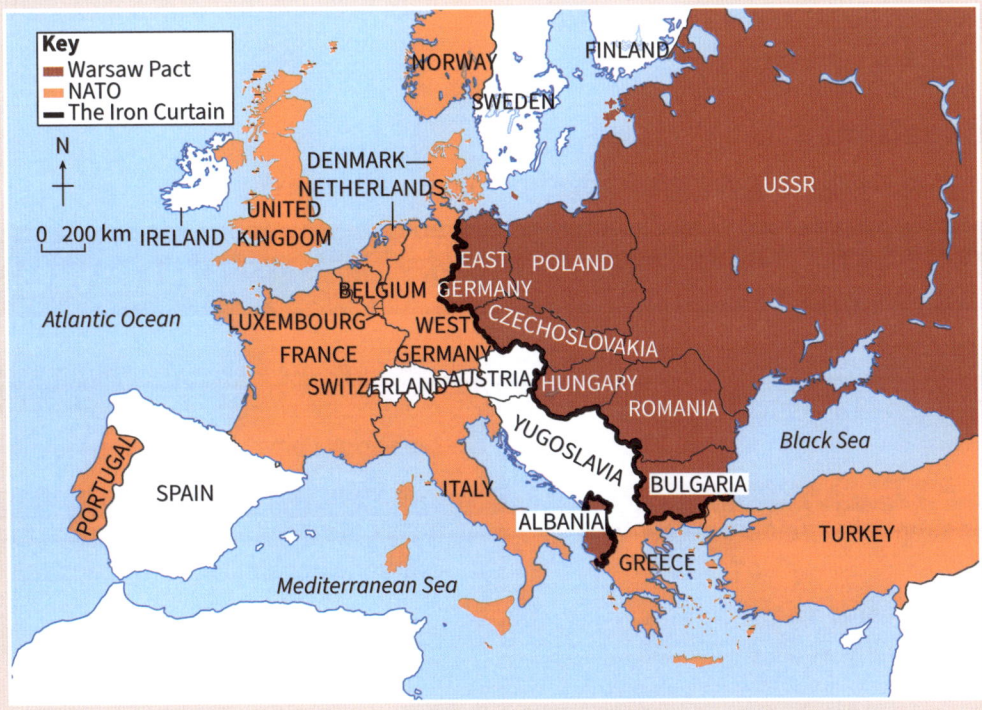

▲ The location of NATO and Warsaw Pact countries in Europe by the end of 1955

Retrieval

Learn the answers to the questions below, then cover the answers column with a piece of paper and write as many as you can. Check and repeat.

Questions | Answers

#	Question	Answer
1	True or false: the Marshall Plan was an economic plan to help European countries recover after the Second World War.	True
2	List two consequences of the Marshall Plan.	Two from: aid allowed many European countries to recover more quickly / the USA had more European trading partners / it demonstrated the USA's support for Europe / it brought Eastern Bloc countries together more closely
3	What was the purpose of Cominform?	It brought the countries of the Eastern bloc together to form one group that followed the policies set by Stalin in Moscow
4	What was the purpose of Comecon?	All member states from Eastern European countries worked together to help each other recover
5	What increased tension in Berlin in 1948?	The USA and Britain combined their zones into Bizonia without consulting the USSR, and they introduced a new currency (the Deutsche Mark)
6	Define the Berlin blockade.	Stalin blocked road, canal, and rail routes into West Berlin, preventing all supplies from reaching West Berlin
7	Define the Berlin airlift.	British and US planes delivered supplies to West Berlin between 26 June and 12 May 1948
8	Name five Western European states that formed NATO along with the USA and Canada in 1949.	Any five from: Britain, France, Denmark, Norway, Italy, Belgium, the Netherlands, Portugal, Luxembourg, and Iceland.

Previous questions

Use the questions below to check your knowledge from previous chapters.

Questions | Answers

#	Question	Answer
1	List two features of a capitalist country.	Two from: privately owned businesses / freedom to make as much money as possible / lots of choice in the shops / big difference between rich and poor
2	List two features of a communist country.	Two from: businesses owned by the government / no private wealth / very little choice in the shops / everyone has similar living standards
3	At which conferences did the Big Three agree that Germany would be divided into four zones?	Yalta Conference, 1945, and Potsdam Conference, 1945

2 The development of the Cold War

Practice 2

Exam-style questions

1. a) Explain **one** consequence of the use of the atomic bombs against Japan in August 1945. (4)

    b) Explain **one** consequence of the creation of the Soviet satellite states in Eastern Europe between 1945 and 1948. (4)

    > **EXAM TIP**
    > The consequences you choose for Questions 1a and 1b could refer to events, decisions or changes in attitude. Whichever consequences you choose, make sure that you include:
    > - detail for each consequence
    > - facts about what happened
    > - the impact of what happened.

2. Write a narrative account analysing the key events leading up to the creation of Comecon by Stalin in 1949. (8)

    > You **may** use the following in your answer:
    > - Marshall Plan
    > - dollar imperialism
    >
    > You **must** also use information of your own.

    > **EXAM TIP**
    > Your answer needs a clear beginning, a middle and an end, and you should write about the events in chronological order. You should include one event of your own. Here, it would seem sensible to choose the Truman Doctrine as the first event.

3. Explain **two** of the following:
    - The importance of Cominform for increasing tension between the superpowers by 1949. (8)

    - The importance of the Truman Doctrine for increased tension between the superpowers by 1948. (8)

    - The importance of the Berlin Blockade for the creation of NATO. (8)

Knowledge

3 The Cold War intensifies

The significance of the arms race

The beginning of the nuclear age

- The USA's use of the atomic bombs against Japan in 1945 increased tension between the superpowers and started a nuclear **arms race**.
- The Soviets successfully tested their own **atomic bomb (A-bomb)** on 29 August 1949.
- The USA responded by building a more advanced hydrogen bomb in 1952.
- The Soviets responded and built their own **hydrogen bomb (H-bomb)** within a year.
- Each side spent huge sums of money on developing nuclear weapons to try to get ahead in the arms race.

Mutually Assured Destruction (MAD)

- No nuclear weapons were launched during the Cold War.
- The knowledge that launching a nuclear weapon would lead to retaliation and, consequently, the destruction of both the USSR and USA, was known as **Mutually Assured Destruction (MAD)**.
- Despite MAD, there were a few occasions when nuclear war looked possible: one crisis point came in 1962, during the Cuban Missile Crisis.

Stepping back from the edge

- After 1962, the arms race slowed down. Both sides realised that a mistake or misunderstanding could lead to nuclear war and annihilation.
- Tensions rose again in the 1980s and spending on arms increased again.
- The presence of nuclear weapons during the Cold War was a concern across the globe.

▲ *The distinctive mushroom-shaped cloud that appeared after the USA dropped the second atomic bomb on Nagasaki, Japan, on 9 August 1945. This caused between 60 000 and 80 000 deaths*

Destalinisation

1. The death of Stalin

- Stalin died in March 1953 and was succeeded by Nikita Khrushchev.
- Khrushchev had been one of Stalin's ministers, and had been responsible for some of the most severe aspects of Stalin's rule.
- However, to the West, Khrushchev seemed more reasonable than Stalin to work with.

▲ Nikita Khrushchev (left), Stalin's successor as leader of the USSR, with President Eisenhower (right) at the White House, Washington DC, in 1959

2. Destalinisation

- In February 1956, Khrushchev **denounced** Stalin's regime as cruel, and announced that a process of **'destalinisation'** would begin.
- Destalinisation included ending Stalin's harshest policies, removing statues and images of Stalin, reducing the size of the secret police, and increasing the number of consumer goods available in the USSR.
- Destalinisation was popular in the USSR, and the West hoped relations between the two superpowers would improve as a result.

3. Impact on the satellite states

- Many people living in the satellite states hoped destalinisation would improve their lives.
- However, Khrushchev realised that allowing the satellite states too much freedom could mean an end to communism in Eastern Europe.
- There was a revolt in Poland against communist rule in June 1956, which was brutally crushed by the USSR.

4. Did superpower relations improve?

- Meetings were held between Khrushchev and US President Eisenhower in 1959.
- Khrushchev talked of a 'peaceful co-existence' between the USSR and the USA.
- However, the arms race continued, with both sides increasing their supply of nuclear weapons.
- The creation of the Warsaw Pact in 1955 was a sign that the USSR felt threatened by the creation of NATO in 1949, suggesting that any improvement in relations was limited.
- Similarly, the American public was fearful of communism and anxious about the spread of communism within the USA.

Key terms — Make sure you can write a definition for these key terms: arms race, atomic bomb (A-bomb), hydrogen bomb (H-bomb), Mutually Assured Destruction (MAD), denounced, destalinisation, purges, reforms, guerrilla tactics

Knowledge

3 The Cold War intensifies

Why did Hungarians want to revolt against communist rule?

- Hungary and Nazi Germany were allies during the Second World War and, in September 1944, the Red Army invaded Hungary.
- In post-war elections in November 1945 in Hungary, the Communist Party won just 17 per cent of the vote but took control of the government.
- By 1947, leaders of non-communist parties in Hungary had been arrested or had fled the country.
- In 1949, Mátyás Rákosi became Hungary's leader, and imposed a pro-Soviet dictatorship.

REVISION TIP

Exam questions often ask you to think about the consequences of something, or its importance. The Berlin Crisis, the arms race, and the Hungarian Uprising are good examples of events where these question types might be asked. Knowing specific details about these will help you access the higher marks in exams.

- 2 000 Hungarians were killed in **purges**.
- The Hungarian secret police used terror to keep people under control.
- There was very little freedom of speech.
- Living standards fell as the economy focused on building weapons, not making consumer goods.

- Students saw Khrushchev's policy of destalinisation as an opportunity to bring **reforms** to Hungary and gain some independence from Soviet control.

The Hungarian Uprising, 1956

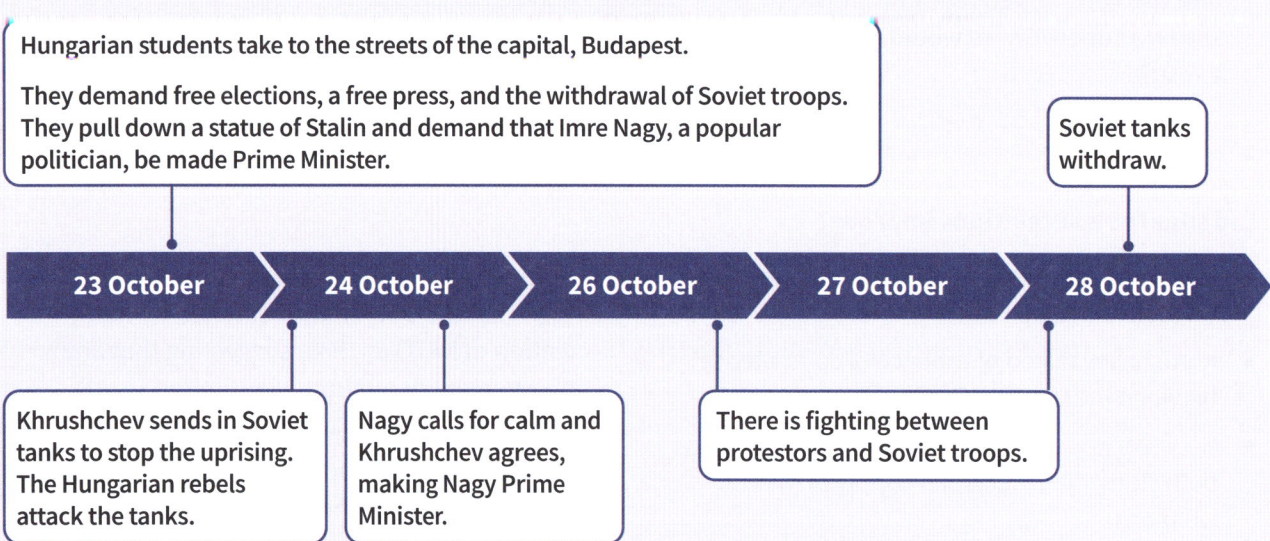

23 October: Hungarian students take to the streets of the capital, Budapest. They demand free elections, a free press, and the withdrawal of Soviet troops. They pull down a statue of Stalin and demand that Imre Nagy, a popular politician, be made Prime Minister.

24 October: Khrushchev sends in Soviet tanks to stop the uprising. The Hungarian rebels attack the tanks.

26 October: Nagy calls for calm and Khrushchev agrees, making Nagy Prime Minister.

27 October: There is fighting between protestors and Soviet troops.

28 October: Soviet tanks withdraw.

As Prime Minister, Nagy announced far-reaching reforms:
- free elections, with other political parties allowed
- freedom of speech and freedom of the press
- Hungary would leave the Warsaw Pact and become a neutral country.

Khrushchev's response

- Nagy's decision to leave the Warsaw Pact went too far for Khrushchev. If Hungary left the Warsaw Pact, other Eastern Bloc countries might follow.
- On 4 November 1956, 6 000 Soviet tanks and 200 000 Soviet troops invaded Budapest.
- Hungarians resisted the invasion using guns and **guerrilla tactics**, ambushing Soviet tanks in the streets.
- It took the USSR two weeks to crush the revolt. Between 3 000 and 20 000 Hungarians, and around 700 Soviet soldiers were killed.

◀ Soviet tanks entered Budapest on 4 November 1956. Many Hungarians fought back using guns

The West's response

Western powers did not help the Hungarians:

- The West was afraid of sending military support to Hungary because Warsaw Pact countries were ready to fight alongside the USSR
- The arms race threatened to turn the dispute into a nuclear war
- World leaders and the United Nations were distracted by the Suez Crisis in Egypt.

However, there was huge public sympathy for the Hungarians in the West, including public demonstrations in Western Europe.

The consequences of the Hungarian Uprising

- 200 000 refugees fled Hungary.
- Nagy was arrested, then later tried and executed by the USSR in 1958.
- János Kádár, a hardline communist, replaced Nagy as Prime Minister. He reversed Nagy's reforms and ensured Hungary was placed back under Soviet control.
- Khrushchev had shown that, despite destalinisation, he was willing to do anything to ensure that the Eastern Bloc remained under Soviet control.
- The USA had shown that it would not interfere with events in the Eastern Bloc.

3 Knowledge

Retrieval

Learn the answers to the questions below, then cover the answers column with a piece of paper and write as many as you can. Check and repeat.

Questions / Answers

#	Question	Answer
1	When did the Soviets successfully test their own A-bomb?	29 August 1949
2	When did each superpower first develop the H-bomb?	The USA in 1952, and the USSR in 1953
3	When did Stalin die and who replaced him as leader of the USSR?	Stalin died in March 1953; Nikita Khrushchev
4	What happened in Poland in 1956?	A revolt against communist rule was brutally crushed by the USSR
5	When did the Hungarian Uprising begin?	23 October 1956
6	What did the students who started the Hungarian Uprising demand?	Free elections / a free press / the withdrawal of Soviet troops / Imre Nagy as Prime Minister
7	What three reforms did Imre Nagy announce when he became Prime Minister of Hungary?	Free elections with other political parties allowed / freedom of speech and freedom of the press / Hungary would leave the Warsaw Pact
8	On what date did Soviet tanks invade Budapest after Nagy became Prime Minister?	4 November 1956
9	How many Soviet tanks and troops invaded Hungary?	6 000 Soviet tanks and 200 000 Soviet troops
10	How long did it take the Soviets to crush the Hungarian Uprising?	Two weeks
11	How many people were killed during the Hungarian Uprising?	Between 3 000 and 20 000 Hungarians, and around 700 Soviet soldiers

Previous questions

Use the questions below to check your knowledge from previous chapters.

#	Question	Answer
1	True or false: the Marshall Plan was an economic plan to help European countries recover after the Second World War.	True
2	What was the purpose of Comecon?	All member states from Eastern European countries worked together to help each other recover
3	Define the Berlin blockade.	Stalin blocked road, canal, and rail routes into West Berlin, preventing all supplies from reaching West Berlin

Practice

Exam-style questions

1. **a)** Explain **one** consequence of Khrushchev's policy of destalinisation in Hungary. **(4)**

   b) Explain **one** consequence of the Hungarian Uprising of 1956. **(4)**

2. Write a narrative account analysing the key events of the arms race between 1945 and 1952. **(8)**

   > You **may** use the following in your answer:
   > - USA developing the atomic bomb
   > - Joseph Stalin
   >
   > You **must** also use information of your own.

   EXAM TIP
   The two bullet points are there to help you find a way into the narrative account, but you don't have to use them. You should try to include at least three events in your answer, though. You could choose to write about the USA's development of the H-bomb in 1952, for example.

3. Explain **two** of the following:
   - The importance of the Yalta Conference in 1945 for increasing tensions between the USA and the USSR. **(8)**

   EXAM TIP
   Your answer needs a clear beginning, middle, and end, and you should write about the events in chronological order. You also need to make links between the events and explain them clearly. Use phrases like, 'This meant that…' and 'This led to…'.

   - The importance of the Long and Novikov telegrams for US–Soviet relations. **(8)**

   - The importance of the creation of the Soviet satellite states in Eastern Europe for East-West relations. **(8)**

Knowledge

4 Cold War crises: Berlin, 1958–61

Why was Berlin a problem?

- Germany's capital city, Berlin, had been divided since 1945.
- The Soviet Union controlled East Berlin.
- The Western allies controlled West Berlin. It was thriving economically behind the Iron Curtain because of the Marshall Plan.
- The Soviet Union saw capitalist West Berlin as an embarrassment, while the West saw it as a success.
- Many East Germans living in Berlin envied the freedoms and wealth enjoyed by West Berliners and hoped to **defect** to West Germany. 100 000 East German refugees crossed the border to West Berlin between 1955 and 1960.
- Many defectors were well educated people like scientists and engineers who performed important jobs. The Soviets wanted to stop this 'brain drain' to the West.

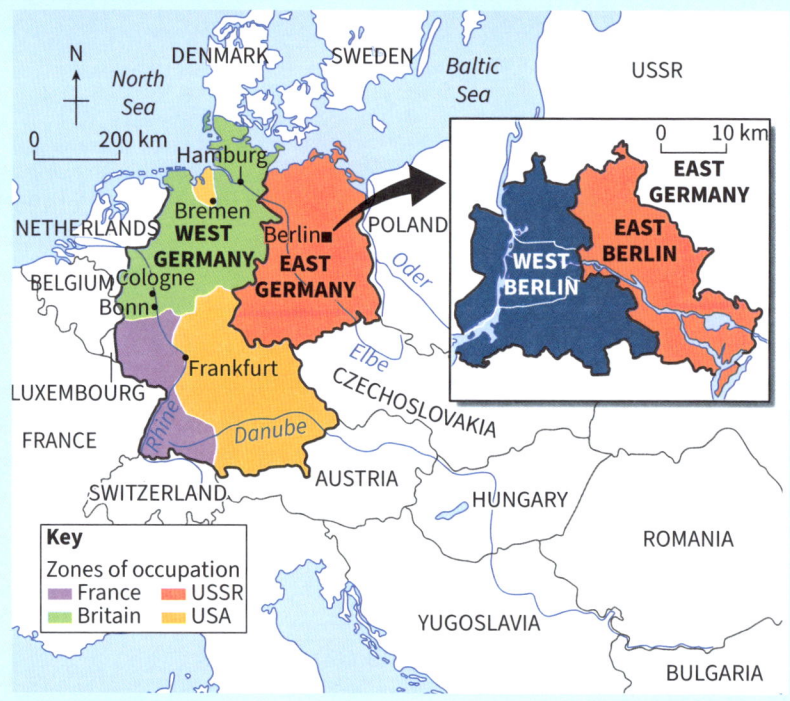

▲ The division of Germany as agreed at the Yalta and Potsdam conferences in 1945

Khrushchev's ultimatum, 1958

- In 1958, Khrushchev described West Berlin as 'a fishbone stuck in our throat'.
- He gave the West an **ultimatum**: withdraw US, British, and French forces from West Berlin within six months.
- This caused tension when the West refused to withdraw.

Summit meetings, 1959–61

May 1959 — Geneva **summit**, Switzerland: Khrushchev meets US President Eisenhower. They fail to resolve the Berlin issue.

1 May 1960 — The Soviets shoot down a US spy plane.

17 May 1960 — Paris summit, France: US President Eisenhower refuses to apologise for the spy plane incident. Khrushchev storms out of the meeting. Problem of Berlin unresolved.

January 1961 — John F. Kennedy becomes US President.

April 1961 — Bay of Pigs: US-backed invasion of communist Cuba ends in failure.

June 1961 — Vienna summit, Austria:
- Khrushchev meets Kennedy for the first time.
- Khrushchev re-issues the Berlin ultimatum.
- Kennedy rejects the ultimatum and increases US defence spending. The Berlin problem remains unresolved.
- Thousands of East German refugees continue to cross into West Berlin.

4

The Berlin Wall

- On 13 August 1961, East German troops closed the border with West Berlin. Soldiers erected a barbed wire barrier encircling the whole of West Berlin, a distance of 43 kilometres.
- Within a week, the barbed wire fence had been replaced with a concrete wall. The Berlin Wall would remain for nearly 30 years.
- The East Germans and Soviets claimed they had built the wall to stop West German spies from entering communist East Germany. In reality, the wall was intended to stop the 'brain drain' of highly educated East German refugees fleeing to West Germany via West Berlin.

▲ *An East German soldier patrols the Berlin Wall, 27 August 1961, as West Berliners look at the new barrier*

Consequences of the Berlin Wall for those living in Germany

- Many Berlin families were now divided and wouldn't see each other until the wall came down in 1989.
- Many East Germans who had hoped to defect to the West had to accept living under communism.
- Some East German refugees still tried to cross the border. In the first year of the wall, 41 East Germans were shot trying to cross to West Germany.

Impact of the Berlin Wall on US–Soviet relations

- US President Kennedy was angered by the wall's construction. However, he realised it had ended the refugee crisis in Berlin, and in this way helped reduce tensions between the USA and USSR.
- However, the East Germans soon started making it very difficult for non-Germans to cross the border in Berlin. This added to tension, as it broke a key agreement of the Yalta Conference of 1945.
- On 28 October 1961, US troops and tanks faced Soviet troops and tanks in a stand-off at **Checkpoint Charlie** – a famous crossing point in the Berlin Wall. The stand-off lasted a few hours, until Kennedy and Khrushchev both agreed to call off their troops.
- In 1963, Kennedy visited West Berlin. Approximately 1.5 million West Berliners lined the streets to greet him. Kennedy made a speech criticising the building of the wall and the communist system in general.
- The Berlin Wall can be seen as a **propaganda** victory for the West: the need to fence in East Berliners was seen as a sign that the Soviet system of communism had failed.

Key terms — Make sure you can write a definition for these key terms: defect   ultimatum   summit   Checkpoint Charlie   propaganda

Retrieval

Learn the answers to the questions below, then cover the answers column with a piece of paper and write as many as you can. Check and repeat.

Questions / Answers

#	Question	Answer
1	What does the term 'defect' mean?	To leave one political system for another
2	The Soviets feared a 'brain drain' as people defected from East to West Berlin. What is a 'brain drain'?	When many skilled people like scientists and engineers leave one country to work in another
3	How many East German refugees crossed the border to West Berlin between 1955 and 1960?	100 000
4	What ultimatum did Khrushchev give the Western allies in 1958 that they ignored?	Withdraw US, British, and French forces from West Berlin within six months.
5	Where did the first summit meeting between Khrushchev and Eisenhower in May 1959 take place?	Geneva, Switzerland
6	What incident, which took place before the Paris summit of 1960, increased tension between the USA and USSR?	The Soviets shot down a US spy plane
7	What was the name of the USA's failed invasion of Cuba in 1961?	Bay of Pigs
8	When was the Berlin Wall erected?	13 August 1961
9	When did US President Kennedy make a speech criticising the building of the Berlin Wall and the communist system in general?	1963

Previous questions

Use the questions below to check your knowledge from previous chapters.

#	Question	Answer
1	List two features of a capitalist country.	Two from: privately owned businesses / freedom to make as much money as possible / lots of choice in the shops / big difference between rich and poor
2	Name five Western European states that formed NATO along with the USA and Canada in 1949.	Any five from: Britain, France, Denmark, Norway, Italy, Belgium, the Netherlands, Portugal, Luxembourg, and Iceland
3	What did the students who started the Hungarian Uprising demand?	Free elections / a free press / the withdrawal of Soviet troops / Imre Nagy as Prime Minister

4 Cold War crises: Berlin, 1958–61

Practice

Exam-style questions

1 **a)** Explain **one** consequence of the ultimatum Khrushchev gave the West in 1958, to withdraw US, British, and French forces from West Berlin within six months. **(4)**

b) Explain **one** consequence of the Berlin Wall being built in 1961. **(4)**

2 Write a narrative account analysing the key developments in relations between the USA and the Soviet Union between 1945 and 1949. **(8)**

> You **may** use the following in your answer:
> - Potsdam Conference
> - Berlin Blockade
>
> You **must** also use information of your own.

EXAM TIP

Identify the focus of the event or development you are being asked to write about. Remember that the two bullet points are there to help you into the narrative account. Make sure you use at least three events in your answer and write about them in the order in which they happened.

3 Explain **two** of the following:
- The importance of the Paris summit of 1960 for relations between the USA and the USSR. **(8)**

- The importance of the refugee crisis for the building of the Berlin Wall in 1961. **(8)**

- The importance of the building of the Berlin Wall for relations between the superpowers. **(8)**

EXAM TIP

These questions are asking you to explain how the event, person, or development in the first part of the question is important to the second part of the question. Use phrases like, 'This was exceedingly important because…', 'This was very important because …', 'This was quite important because…', 'This meant…'

4 Practice

Knowledge

5 Cold War crises: Cuba

Revolution in Cuba

- **1933**: Since 1933, Cuba has been ruled by a corrupt and often brutal government led by Fulgencio Batista. Batista becomes wealthy doing deals with US businessmen, while the people of Cuba remain poor.
- **1950**: By the 1950s, many Cubans have begun to challenge Batista's regime. A young lawyer called Fidel Castro calls for revolution and is exiled.
- **1953**: Castro is ordered to leave Cuba.
- **1956**: Castro and 81 supporters return to Cuba and begin a two-year guerrilla war against the government. Castro's support grows.
- **1959**: On 1 January, Batista flees Cuba and Castro takes power.

Castro's communist revolution

- Castro never talked about communism, yet his political beliefs were left wing.
- Castro's government took many of Cuba's industries into state ownership. Some of these industries were owned by Americans.
- Castro was keen to work with Americans and visited the USA shortly after becoming leader in 1959. However, President Eisenhower refused to meet him.
- As the USA was unwilling to work with Castro, he turned to the USSR, which provided loans and oil to Cuba.
- In response, in 1961, the USA placed an **embargo** on Cuba. This increased Cuba's reliance on the USSR.

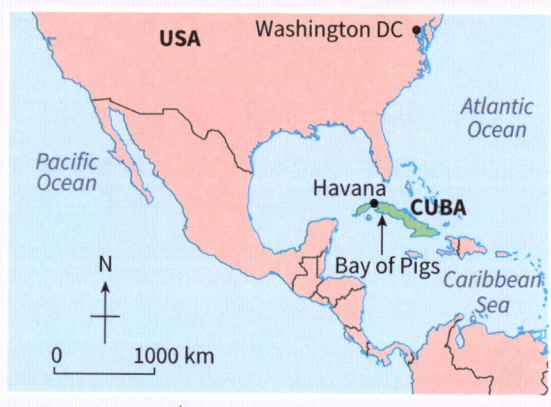

▲ *The location of Cuba*

Bay of Pigs, 1961

The plan	The invasion	Consequences for Cuba
The CIA drew up a plan to help Castro's exiled opponents re-take Cuba. Exiles would land at the Bay of Pigs. Under US air force cover they would march 70km to the capital and take Havana, gaining support on the way.	Prior to the invasion, the new President Kennedy withdrew the support of the US air force, worried about international reaction. The invasion went ahead on 17 April. Without aircover the exiles were left exposed; 200 were killed and many more were captured. No Cubans turned out to support the invasion.	Castro had won a great victory, but he knew that the USA would not give up and Cuba remained vulnerable. The Bay of Pigs incident pushed Cuba closer to the USSR and tensions between the superpowers increased.

Consequences for the USA

Despite the lack of US planes, it was obvious the USA had broken international law and had been made to look weak.

President Kennedy appeared inexperienced when dealing with superpower relations.

The Cuban Missile Crisis, 1962

- After the Bay of Pigs invasion, Khrushchev had a communist ally in Cuba, just 150 km from the US coast.
- Khrushchev wanted to put nuclear weapons close to the USA, as there were already US nuclear weapons in Turkey, near the USSR.

Key terms — Make sure you can write a definition for these key terms

embargo   quarantine   brinkmanship   hotline

26 October
The USA prepares for a possible invasion of Cuba. 120 000 US troops assemble in Florida.
Kennedy receives a telegram from Khrushchev saying he will remove all missiles from Cuba if the USA agrees not to invade Cuba.

27 October
Khrushchev sends a second telegram to Kennedy, again promising to remove missiles from Cuba. Khrushchev also demands that US missiles are removed from Turkey and Italy.
Kennedy agrees to Khrushchev's demands so long as the removal of US missiles is kept secret.

23 October
Soviet ships approach Cuba carrying missiles. The crisis is now a game of **brinkmanship**.

14 October
The USA discovers nuclear weapons bases in Cuba.

> Rising tensions → The brink of war → Closer to the brink → Crisis averted

21 October
Kennedy introduces a **quarantine** zone and a blockade of Cuba by the US navy, aimed at stopping all ships from reaching the island.
Khrushchev begins preparations to defend Cuba if the USA invades.

24 October
The Secretary General of the UN calls for calm. Khrushchev orders his ships to stop.

25 October
7:15am: a Soviet ship enters the quarantine zone. It is stopped by the USA but allowed to pass as it is an oil tanker.

27 October
The USA discovers a Soviet submarine carrying nuclear missiles close to Cuba. The submarine has lost contact with the Soviet navy.
The Cuban government shoots down a US spy plane.
A second US spy plane flees Soviet airspace in Alaska.

The consequences of the Cuban Missile Crisis

Consequences for the USSR	Consequences for the USA	Consequences for the world

• Cuba and the USSR remained allies.
• The removal of US nuclear weapons from Turkey and Italy was a major victory for Khrushchev, but he could not claim credit for it.
• Senior Soviet officials thought Khrushchev handled the crisis badly and this led to his removal from power in 1964.
	• Kennedy showed that he could stand up to the Soviets and was a tough negotiator.
	• The potential nuclear threat to the USA had been removed.
		• A **hotline** was created between the USA and the USSR to avoid future misunderstandings.
		• Both superpowers now wanted to slow the arms race. They agreed:
		  – The Limited Test Ban Treaty (1963)
		  – The Outer Space Treaty (1967)
		  – The Nuclear Non-Proliferation Treaty (1968).

Retrieval

Learn the answers to the questions below, then cover the answers column with a piece of paper and write as many as you can. Check and repeat.

Questions / Answers

#	Question	Answer
1	Why was Cuban lawyer Fidel Castro exiled from Cuba in 1953?	He called for a revolution
2	Why did Fidel Castro look to work closely with the Soviet Union in 1959?	The USA refused to work with Cuba fearing it was communist
3	What was the USA's plan for the Bay of Pigs operation?	The exiles would land at the Bay of Pigs. The CIA would help Castro's exiled opponents re-take Cuba
4	True or false: the Bay of Pigs operation was a huge success for the USA.	False: it was a disaster
5	Why did Khruschev want to put nuclear weapons close to the USA?	There were already US nuclear weapons in Turkey, near the USSR
6	What was the aim of the US military blockade of Cuba, introduced on 21 October 1963?	To stop all Soviet ships from reaching Cuba
7	Which superpower leader sent two telegrams to President Kennedy agreeing to remove nuclear weapons from Cuba?	Khrushchev
8	What was created between the USA and the USSR to avoid misunderstandings in the future?	A hotline
9	What was the aim of the Nuclear Non-Proliferation Treaty of 1968?	To slow the arms race

Previous questions

Use the questions below to check your knowledge from previous chapters.

#	Question	Answer
1	The Soviets feared a 'brain drain' as people defected from East to West Berlin. What is a 'brain drain'?	When many skilled people like doctors and scientists leave one country to work in another
2	What ultimatum did Khrushchev give the Western allies in 1958 that they ignored?	Withdraw US, British, and French forces from West Berlin within six months. They refused to withdraw
3	When was the Berlin Wall first erected?	13 August 1961

5 Cold War crises: Cuba

Practice

Exam-style questions

1 **a)** Explain **one** consequence of the Truman Doctrine. (4)

b) Explain **one** consequence of the Marshall Plan. (4)

> **EXAM TIP**
> Remember to include your own contextual knowledge to explain the consequence. For example, if you say that the consequence of the Truman Doctrine was the creation of Cominform, then you should also explain what Cominform was and why it was created.

2 Write a narrative account analysing the key events of the Bay of Pigs incident (1961). (8)

> You **may** use the following in your answer:
> - President Kennedy
> - exiles
>
> You **must** also use information of your own.

> **EXAM TIP**
> Identify the person, event or development covered in the bullet point. Then think about the importance of that event, person or development in both the short-term and the longer term. Also remember to include facts to support the point you are making.

3 Explain **two** of the following:
- The importance of the Cuban Revolution for superpower relations. (8)

- The importance of the Bay of Pigs incident (1961) for East–West relations. (8)

- The importance of the Cuban Missile Crisis (1962) for reducing tensions between the superpowers. (8)

Knowledge

6 Cold War crises: the Prague Spring

Life before the Prague Spring

- Like other countries behind the Iron Curtain, Czechoslovakia was under the control of the USSR. Czechoslovakia was a one-party communist state. No opposition was allowed, and the press and media were tightly controlled.
- By the 1960s, economic problems were mounting in Czechoslovakia. People's lives were hard and the country's leader Antonín Novotný was corrupt and unpopular.
- An economist named Ota Šik called for reforms including giving ordinary people more power and allowing private business to exist. While Šik's ideas inspired some Czechoslovakians, the USSR rejected his ideas.

▲ The location of Czechoslovakia within the Eastern Bloc

Dubček's reforms

- In January 1968, Novotný was forced to resign. He was replaced as leader by Alexander Dubček.
- Dubček introduced reforms, which were called '**socialism** with a human face' – in other words, they were a form of communism that was considered kinder to the people. They included:
  - allowing Czechoslovakians to run their own businesses
  - allowing public meetings and freedom of speech
  - ending press censorship
  - giving people the right to visit non-communist countries
  - allowing trade unions and other political groups to form.
- Although unhappy with the reforms, Moscow allowed them to go ahead. This encouraged more reforms from Dubček. All these changes became known as the Prague Spring.

▲ Alexander Dubček became Czechoslovakian leader in 1968. He introduced reforms known as the Prague Spring

The Soviet response to the Prague Spring

- The Prague Spring represented the first real challenge to Leonid Brezhnev, the new leader of the USSR.
- Students in Poland were inspired by Dubček's reforms. Therefore, leaders of other Eastern Bloc countries were concerned about events in Czechoslovakia.
- In June 1968, Warsaw Pact countries chose Czechoslovakia's border as a site for Warsaw Pact military exercises. This was designed to intimidate Dubček.
- In July 1968, Warsaw Pact countries met without Czechoslovakia and issued the Warsaw Letter demanding that Dubček back down from his reforms.
- Brezhnev met with Dubček, but Dubček wouldn't halt his reforms.
- On 26 August 1968, Soviet tanks entered Czechoslovakia and quickly took control of the capital, Prague. The Prague Spring was over.

International reactions to the Prague Spring

Inside the Warsaw Pact 	While the governments of other Warsaw Pact countries were supportive of the Soviet invasion of Czechoslovakia, many ordinary people protested it. There was even a protest in Red Square in Moscow. The biggest threat came from the Red Army. Soviet soldiers had been told that the invasion of Czechoslovakia had been requested by the Czechoslovakian people. When the Red Army arrived, this clearly was not the case. Returning soldiers shared their stories with their families and this damaged the reputation of Soviet leaders.
China 	China was the most powerful communist country outside of Eastern Europe. China reacted negatively to the Soviet invasion of Czechoslovakia, and relations between the USSR and China were damaged by the Prague Spring. The Chinese claimed that the Soviets were abandoning communism.
The Western response 	The USA condemned the invasion and cancelled an upcoming meeting between President Johnson and Brezhnev. However, the USA did not want to risk escalating tensions behind the Iron Curtain too much, as they were more pre-occupied with the war in Vietnam. Other Western European countries also reacted negatively and criticised the invasion.

The Brezhnev Doctrine

- In November 1968, Soviet leader Brezhnev gave a speech outlining his approach to any future challenges to Soviet-controlled Eastern Europe.
- He made it clear that if any country followed the example of Czechoslovakia, it would face the same consequences.
- This policy became known as the Brezhnev Doctrine.

REVISION TIP

You will again notice an emphasis on the importance and consequences of events such as the Prague Spring. Make sure that 'importance' and 'consequences' are a focus for your revision.

International reactions to the Brezhnev Doctrine

- The USA initially reacted negatively, calling off talks intended to improve relations between the USSR and the USA. However, the USA quickly changed its mind so they wouldn't undo the progress made since the Cuban Missile Crisis.
- The Chinese regarded the Brezhnev Doctrine with suspicion, thinking the Soviets might invade China, too. As a result, relations between the two communist superpowers soured.

 **Key term** Make sure you can write a definition for this key term — socialism

Retrieval

Learn the answers to the questions below, then cover the answers column with a piece of paper and write as many as you can. Check and repeat.

Questions | Answers

#	Questions	Answers
1	Which Czechoslovakian economist called for reforms including allowing private business to exist?	Ota Šik
2	How did the USSR respond to Ota Šik's calls for reform?	The USSR rejected his ideas
3	Who replaced Novotný as leader of Czechoslovakia in 1968?	Dubček
4	What was the phrase used to describe the sweeping reforms Dubček called for?	'Socialism with a human face'
5	Identify two features of the Prague Spring.	Two from: allowing Czechoslovakians to run their own businesses / allowing freedom of speech / ending censorship / allowing freedom to visit other countries / allowing trade unions and other political parties
6	Who was leader of the USSR during the Prague Spring?	Brezhnev
7	Who was the 'Warsaw Letter' from and what did it demand?	It was from the Warsaw Pact countries and it demanded a stop to Dubček's reforms
8	How did the USSR end the Prague Spring?	By sending tanks into Prague in August 1968
9	How did some citizens within the USSR respond to the Soviet invasion of Czechoslovakia?	Many ordinary people protested about the invasion
10	What was the Brezhnev Doctrine?	A speech in which Brezhnev stated that any other Eastern Bloc country following Czechoslovakia's example would face the same consequences

Previous questions

Use the questions below to check your knowledge from previous chapters.

#	Questions	Answers
1	What two events are considered as important reasons for the start of the Cold War?	The USA's development of the atomic bomb; the establishment of the Eastern Bloc
2	What was the aim of the US military blockade of Cuba, introduced on 21 October 1963?	To stop all Soviet ships from reaching Cuba
3	What was the aim of the Nuclear Non-Proliferation Treaty of 1968?	To stop other countries getting nuclear weapons

6 Cold War crises: the Prague Spring

Practice

6

Exam-style questions

1 **a)** Explain **one** consequence of Alexander Dubček becoming Czechoslovakian leader in 1968. **(4)**

b) Explain **one** consequence of the Prague Spring. **(4)**

2 Write a narrative account analysing the key events of the Prague Spring (1968). **(8)**

You **may** use the following in your answer:
- Warsaw Pact military exercises
- Soviet invasion of Prague

You **must** also use information of your own.

> **EXAM TIP**
> Think about your answer as a story. It needs a beginning, a middle, and an end. The two bullet points will only hint at part of the story. Use your knowledge to ensure that you cover the whole story.

3 Explain **two** of the following:
- The importance of the policy of destalinisation for US–Soviet relations. **(8)**

- The importance of the policy of Mutually Assured Destruction for relations between the superpowers. **(8)**

- The importance of the Hungarian Uprising of 1956 for East–West relations. **(8)**

> **EXAM TIP**
> The question contains three bullet points, and you must choose two to write about in the exam. Read all three bullet points carefully before circling the two you think you can answer best.

6 Practice   **31**

Knowledge

7 Changing relationship between the superpowers

Reasons for Détente in the 1970s

By the early 1970s, both the USA and the USSR saw the benefits of reducing tension and developing a friendlier relationship. There were several reasons why each side wanted **Détente**:

1. Economic reasons
- The huge cost of the Cold War meant standards of living were falling in both the USA and USSR.
- Reducing tension would allow the Eastern Bloc to trade with the West.

2. Vietnam War
- The Vietnam War showed that nuclear weapons did not help win conventional wars.
- Vietnam was expensive for the USA. The war also caused protests at home and abroad.

3. Tensions between the USSR and China
- Tensions increased between the USSR and China.
- The USA tried to build trust with China. This worried the Soviets, who sought to be on friendlier terms with the West.

4. No end in sight to the Cold War
- By the early 1970s, the Cold War had been going for almost 25 years. Both sides were more willing to accept each other's spheres of influence.

5. The Nixon Doctrine
- Richard Nixon, US President 1969–74, stated the USA would no longer support its allies militarily. This change reflected the huge costs of Vietnam.
- Nixon sought better relations with the USSR and met Brezhnev several times.

Strategic Arms Limitation Talks (SALT), 1972

The USSR and USA agreed to:
- ✓ freeze the number of submarine-launched ballistic missiles
- ✓ reduce the number of anti-**ballistic missile** sites.
- ✗ However, both sides could keep their stockpiles of existing weapons.

The Helsinki Accords, 1975

At this summit in Finland, 35 countries, including the USSR and the USA, agreed to:
- ✓ improve human rights, allowing freedom of speech, press, religion, and movement
- ✓ recognise the borders of Eastern Europe, created by the Soviets in 1945
- ✓ improve economic and scientific co-operation between East and West.
- ✗ However, many agreements were broken and human rights did not improve in the USSR.

The failure of SALT

- ✗ The USA and the USSR continued to develop and stockpile nuclear weapons.
- ✗ New weapons technology meant the specific terms of SALT were soon out of date.
- ✗ In 1978, President Carter increased the US defence budget.
- ✗ Brezhnev had placed 2 000 Soviet troops in Cuba by 1979.

→

SALT II (1979)

Brezhnev and US President Jimmy Carter agreed to:

- ✓ limit the delivery and placement of nuclear weapons
- ✓ ban the new and improved ICBMs (intercontinental ballistic missiles)
- ✓ restrict the use of missile launchers and bomber aircraft.
- ✗ However, Soviet leaders and the US Senate refused to approve the treaty.

The Soviet invasion of Afghanistan, 1979

- Afghanistan lies between the 'oil rich' Middle East and the USSR.
- Iran's 1979 Revolution introduced strict laws limiting individual freedoms. The Soviets worried that Soviet Muslims might want to do something similar.
- In September 1979, a communist, Hafizullah Amin, seized power in Afghanistan. He was unpopular with Afghan Muslims.
- Some Afghan Muslims joined a guerrilla fighting force called the **Mujahideen** and opposed Amin's government. This made Afghanistan very unstable.
- Brezhnev decided to act: the USSR invaded Afghanistan on 25 December 1979.
- Soviet troops quickly captured the capital, Kabul. Amin was killed and replaced by pro-Soviet leader Babrak Karmal.
- Many Afghan soldiers deserted and joined the Mujahideen to fight against the Soviet invasion.

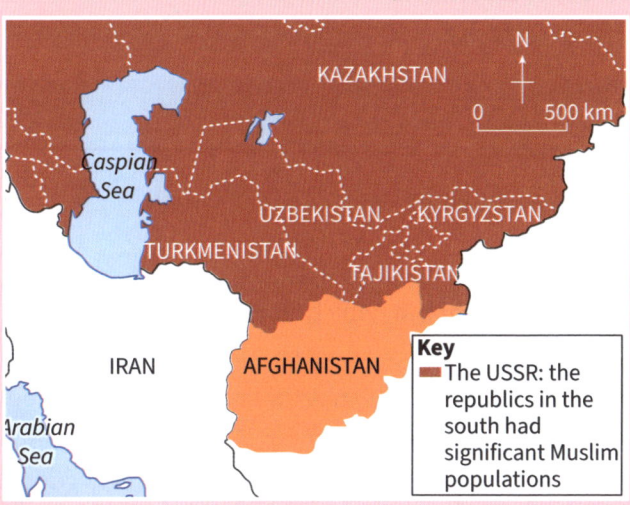

▲ *The location of Afghanistan*

- The Soviets sent 85 000 troops to Afghanistan to keep Karmal in power. Soviet troops remained there until 1989.

↓

The consequences of the Soviet invasion of Afghanistan

The Carter Doctrine	The end of Détente	The Olympic Boycotts
US President Jimmy Carter declared the Soviet invasion a threat to world peace and established the Carter Doctrine which: • created a Rapid Deployment Force to move troops quickly to the area AND sent the navy to the Arabian Sea • allowed Afghanistan's neighbours to receive military aid.	• SALT II was never formally agreed by the US government. • Key trade agreements between the USA and USSR were abandoned. • The USA armed and funded the Mujahideen. • Détente ended.	• Carter pressured the USA to withdraw from the 1980 Moscow Olympic Games, which 61 other countries also **boycotted**. • The Soviets boycotted the 1984 Olympics in Los Angeles, USA. 13 Eastern Bloc countries also withdrew their athletes.

Knowledge

7 Changing relationship between the superpowers

The election of US President Ronald Reagan, 1980

- The war in Afghanistan showed the USSR was not committed to Détente.
- Many US voters thought President Carter's approach to the USSR had been too soft and had weakened the USA.
- US voters turned to presidential candidate Ronald Reagan, who was highly critical of the USSR and promised to be much tougher when dealing with the Soviets.
- Reagan defeated Carter in the November 1980 US presidential election.
- Reagan's election marked the beginning of what is known as the **Second Cold War**.

Reagan's policies

Soon after Reagan was elected, US spending on defence increased by 13 per cent.

The US developed new weapons including:

- a **neutron bomb** (which could kill huge numbers of people)
- stealth bombers (planes that could fly undetected).

In 1983, Reagan described the USSR as an 'evil empire', relating the New Cold War to a battle between 'good and evil', like in the Star Wars films.

Reagan announced the **Strategic Defence Initiative (SDI)**, which became known as the Star Wars programme.

SDI would detect and destroy missiles using laser technology before they could reach the USA. It was never completed, but the idea of SDI increased tension with the USSR.

▲ Ronald Reagan

> **REVISION TIP**
>
> Why not prepare short fact files on some of the Cold War's 'big names' – e.g., Reagan, Brezhnev, Nixon, and Dubček? Familiarity with some personal details and the roles people played can help to make better sense of the topics.

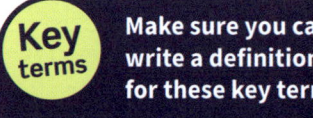 Make sure you can write a definition for these key terms

Détente   ballistic missile   Mujahideen   boycott
Second Cold War   neutron bomb
Strategic Defence Initiative (SDI)   glasnost   perestroika

Urgent problems for Soviet leader Mikhail Gorbachev

When he came to power in 1985, the new leader of the USSR, Mikhail Gorbachev faced three urgent problems.

1. Most industries in the USSR were using old machinery and outdated methods, so production of household goods was slow. This meant standards of living were much poorer than they were in the West.
2. During Détente, Eastern Bloc countries had traded with and borrowed money from the West. They now struggled to pay this money back.
3. The Second Cold War and Reagan's SDI led to a new arms race with the USA, which the USSR simply could not afford.

▲ *Mikhail Gorbachev.*

Gorbachev's 'new thinking'

To help solve the problems facing the USSR and the Eastern Bloc, Gorbachev applied 'new thinking'. This new thinking included:

Glasnost meaning 'openness'

Aimed to:
- allow people to openly express new ideas that were different from the government's
- restore public trust in the communist leadership, which had previously punished people for speaking out against the regime.

Perestroika meaning 'restructuring'

Aimed to change the economy by:
- encouraging more involvement by foreign businesses
- allowing businesses, not the government, to respond to customer demand.

Gorbachev's impact on superpower relations

- Gorbachev's 'new thinking' convinced President Reagan that he might be able to work with the USSR to try and slow or stop the new arms race.
- The two leaders met three times: in 1985 in Switzerland; in 1986 in Iceland; in 1987 in Washington DC.
- At the Washington summit, the USA and USSR agreed to the Intermediate-Range Nuclear Forces Treaty (INF). Whereas previous treaties had been about arms control, this was about arms reduction. Both sides promised to get rid of all medium- and short-range nuclear weapons.

Retrieval

Learn the answers to the questions below, then cover the answers column with a piece of paper and write as many as you can. Check and repeat.

	Questions	Answers
1	What does SALT stand for?	Strategic Arms Limitation Talks
2	What did the USA and the USSR agree at SALT (1972)?	To freeze number of submarine-launched ballistic missiles / to reduce number of anti-ballistic missile sites
3	Which superpower leaders met in 1979 at the SALT II talks?	Brezhnev and Carter
4	What did the USA and the USSR agree at SALT II?	To limit delivery and placement of nuclear weapons / to ban ICBMs / to restrict use of missile launchers and bomber aircraft
5	Who seized power in Afghanistan in September 1979?	Communist leader Hafizullah Amin
6	State three consequences of the Soviet invasion of Afghanistan on East–West relations.	President Carter introduced the Carter Doctrine to defend US interests in the Middle East / the end of Détente / Olympic boycotts – of the USSR in 1980 and the USA in 1984
7	Who became US President in 1981?	Reagan
8	Who became Soviet leader in 1985?	Gorbachev
9	What terms described the USSR's new policies of 'openness' and 're-structuring'?	*Glasnost* and *perestroika*

Previous questions

Use the questions below to check your knowledge from previous chapters.

	Questions	Answers
1	Which group of countries formed NATO?	The USA and countries in Western Europe
2	What three reforms did Imre Nagy announce when he became Prime Minister of Hungary?	Free elections with other political parties allowed / freedom of speech and freedom of the press / Hungary would leave the Warsaw Pact
3	What ultimatum did Khrushchev give the Western allies in 1958?	Withdraw US, British, and French forces from West Berlin within six months

7 Changing relationship between the superpowers

Practice

Exam-style questions

1. **a)** Explain **one** consequence of the Bay of Pigs invasion in 1961. **(4)**

   b) Explain **one** consequence of the Cuban Missile Crisis of 1962. **(4)**

2. Write a narrative account analysing the main events in superpower relations during Détente, between 1972 and 1979. **(8)**

   You **may** use the following in your answer:
   - Vietnam
   - SALT treaties

   You **must** also use information of your own.

   > **EXAM TIP**
   > When answering this question, make sure you describe the main events of Détente in chronological order. Aim to include the years in which each of the events took place, too. This will make you look knowledgeable to the examiner.

3. Explain **two** of the following:
   - The importance of the Helsinki Accords for relations between the two superpowers. **(8)**
   - The importance of the Soviet invasion of Afghanistan for East–West relations. **(8)**
   - The importance of Reagan's Strategic Defence Initiative for relations between the USA and the USSR in the 1980s. **(8)**

   > **EXAM TIP**
   > These questions are asking you to explain the key reasons why an event or a trend happened. So, keep a tight focus on how the importance of the first development helped cause the second. Use phrases like, 'This was very important…', 'This was exceedingly important…', 'This was quite important…', 'This was because…', 'This meant…'

Knowledge

8 The collapse of the USSR

The loosening grip of the USSR on Eastern Europe

- In the mid-1980s, Soviet leader Mikhail Gorbachev abandoned the Brezhnev Doctrine and loosened Soviet control of the Eastern Bloc.
- Gorbachev's policy was dubbed the **Sinatra Doctrine** – after the song 'My Way' by the American singer Frank Sinatra. The Sinatra Doctrine allowed countries to rule in their own way without Soviet interference.
- Gorbachev hoped to strengthen communism by giving people more freedom and **democracy**. However, many people in Eastern Europe were fed up with poor living conditions and limited freedom, and wanted change.

The collapse of Soviet control of Eastern Europe

East Germany
Demonstrations across East Germany in late 1989 called for reforms. On 9 November 1989, the border in Berlin was opened and thousands of East Germans crossed into West Berlin, many taking hammers and axes to smash the Berlin Wall. In the weeks that followed, communism collapsed in East Germany. On 3 October 1990, West and East Germany were reunited as one country.

Poland
In 1988, there were strikes across Poland and workers formed their own trade union called **Solidarity**. Solidarity's leader Lech Wałęsa met with communist leaders and a free election was held in June 1989. The communists lost and, in August 1989, Poland became a non-communist country.

Hungary
Communist leaders in Hungary introduced reforms including a free press in late 1988. In June 1989, there was a free election. In August 1989, the border with Austria was opened allowing people to travel. On 23 October 1989, the communist government officially came to an end.

Czechoslovakia
Demonstrations and strikes took place in November 1989. The communist government realised they had lost control. They gave up power and announced free elections, which took place in June 1990. The Velvet Revolution (so-called because of how calmly it played out) was almost entirely peaceful.

Romania
Protests began in 1989. The Romanian government under Nicolae Ceaușescu brutally put down these protests: soldiers shot protesters. Then, on 22 December, the military joined the protests and Ceaușescu lost power. Free elections were held on 20 May 1990. However, Romania continued to face violent unrest for several years.

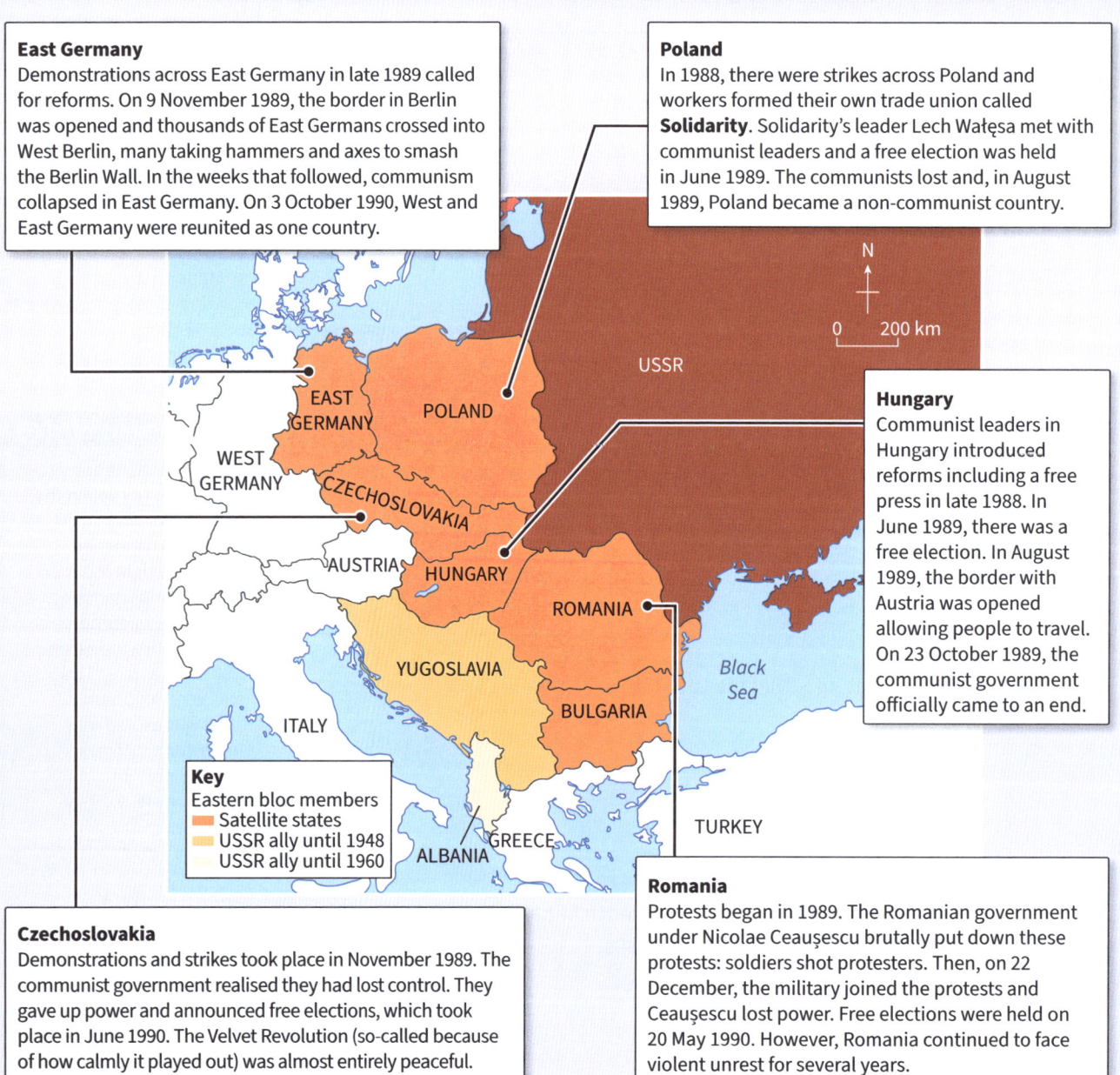

▲ Map of Eastern Europe

8 The collapse of the USSR

The collapse of Soviet control of Eastern Europe

- The speed at which countries in Eastern Europe abandoned communism undermined the power and control of the USSR. It also undermined Gorbachev's position as Soviet leader.
- It proved to the USA that communism had only survived due to force and control.
- It led to concern in the West that there might be a power vacuum in Eastern Europe. Who might take control? Would there be civil wars? Would the new countries work together?

The significance of the fall of the Berlin Wall

East Germany was slow to embrace Gorbachev's 'new thinking', partly because the government banned some Soviet publications in the late 1980s.

→ Many East Germans were buoyed by Eastern Bloc countries abandoning communism in the summer of 1989 and started demonstrations in East Germany.

→ After the Hungarian government opened the border with Austria in August 1989, many East Germans escaped to West Germany via Czechoslovakia, Hungary, and Austria with no opposition.

On 9 November 1989, the East German government relented and announced that the border between East and West Berlin would be opened. Within a few days, 1 million East Germans had crossed the border, visiting relatives in West Berlin for the first time in 28 years and enjoying the relative freedom and prosperity of life in the West.

← On 4 November 1989, a million East Germans attended a demonstration in East Berlin to demand democracy. This led East Germany's communist leaders to announce some limited freedoms to travel.

← East German communist leader Erich Honecker hoped for Soviet intervention but was disappointed when Gorbachev visited East Germany in October 1989. Gorbachev refused to get involved in East Germany's affairs.

- The fall of the Berlin Wall is seen by many historians as the final major event of the Cold War. It showed that the USSR had given up control of Eastern Europe and the **Warsaw Pact**, and was no longer willing to have influence there.
- Although communism in the USSR continued for another two years, when the Berlin Wall came down on 9 November 1989, the end of the Cold War appeared inevitable.

▶ East and West Germans gather on top of the Berlin Wall on 9 November 1989. One is using a pick axe to smash it

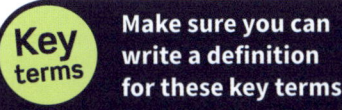 **Key terms** Make sure you can write a definition for these key terms

Sinatra Doctrine   democracy   Solidarity   Warsaw Pact   coup

Knowledge

8 The collapse of the USSR

The collapse of the USSR

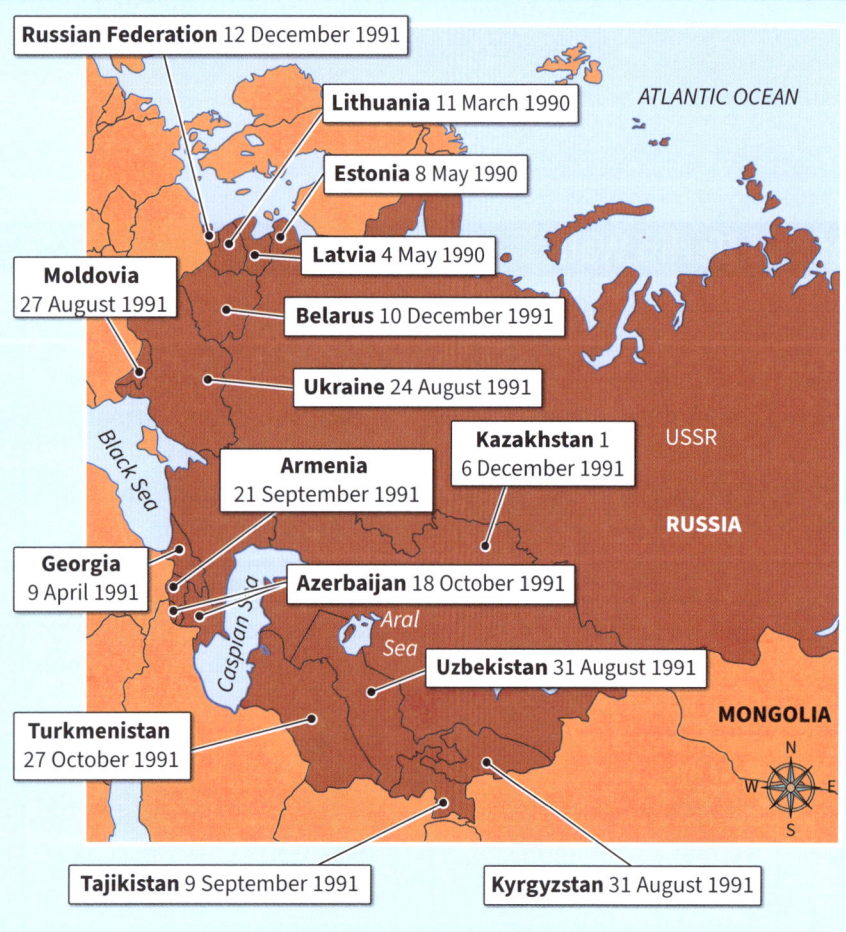

▲ The 15 states of the USSR and when they formally declared independence

- The end of communist rule across Eastern Europe in 1989–90 was a huge blow to Soviet leaders. Leading members of the Communist Party of the Soviet Union became increasingly worried about the impact of Gorbachev's policies on the USSR. Eastern Europe had been lost – and it now looked like the USSR would also disintegrate.

- The USSR was made up of 15 different republics, including Russia. Inspired by what had happened in Eastern Europe, the non-Russian parts of the USSR started to call for more independence. In March 1990, Lithuania left the USSR. Estonia and Latvia soon joined them.

> **REVISION TIP**
>
> Learning specific, factual details (such as how many republics made up the USSR) can really help lift vague exam answers and gain you marks.

Gorbachev loses power, 1991

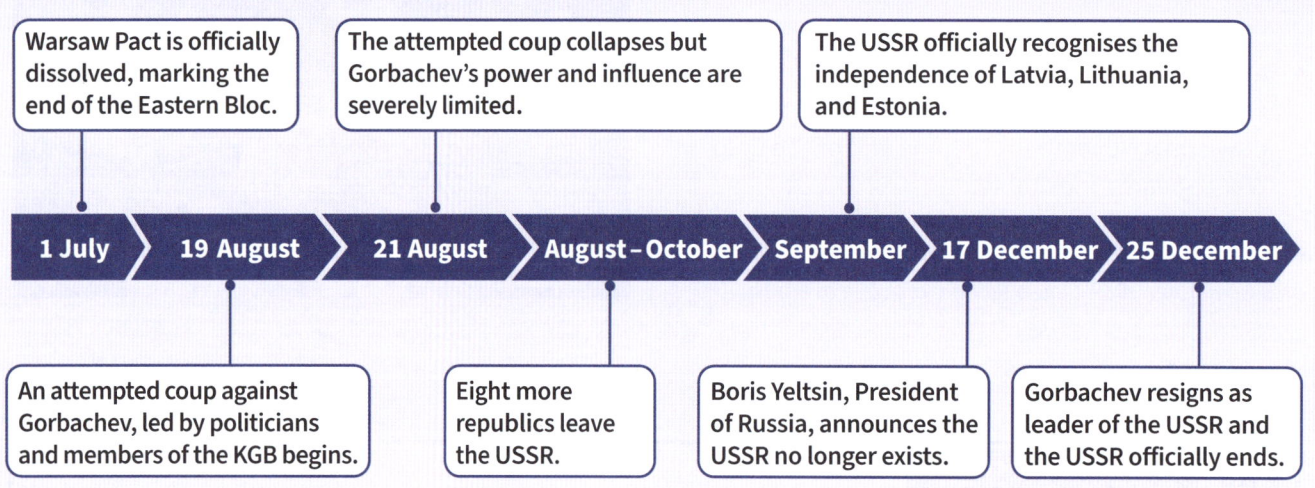

An attempted coup

- In August 1991, a group of politicians and members of the KGB attempted to take control in a **coup** and remove Gorbachev from power.
- However, the coup had little support. Boris Yeltsin, Mayor of Moscow, refused to support the new government. Yeltsin called for the people to resist the new regime. Soldiers who had been sent to arrest Yeltsin, joined the protestors in Moscow and the coup failed.

The end of the Cold War

- By the end of 1991, the Cold War was over. The USA remained the world's only superpower.
- The USA now had to worry about the actions of many governments rather than just about the actions of the USSR.
- Most concerning for the USA was the huge stockpiles of nuclear weapons spread across the former USSR. Would they end up in the hands of less predictable leaders?

Why did the Cold War end?

Historians disagree on exactly why the Cold War ended but it certainly happened very quickly.

Reasons why the Cold War ended

Mikhail Gorbachev
- Became leader of the USSR in 1985.
- Aimed to save the Soviet economy and reform the country without abandoning communism.
- Gave Eastern Bloc countries more say in how their countries were run, so many declared themselves independent.
- Improved relations with the West, weakened the Eastern Bloc and ended hostilities with the USA.

The collapse of the Warsaw Pact
The two superpowers relied on their allies to increase their power. When the USSR's allies abandoned communism, the Warsaw Pact was dissolved, leaving the USSR severely weakened.

The attempted August 1991 coup
- Left Gorbachev in a weak position and the USSR on the verge of collapse.
- Lithuania declared independence in March 1990 and, by the end of 1991, all the other Soviet Republics had done the same.
- Gorbachev had little power when Yeltsin declared the USSR would cease to exist in December 1991.

Soviet economic weakness
- By the 1980s, Soviet living standards were falling and goods made in the Eastern Bloc were of a poor standard.
- The USSR government could not keep up with US spending on the arms race.

Ronald Reagan
- Increased pressure on the USSR by re-igniting the arms race; the USA increased spending on weapons, including the proposed Strategic Defence Initiative.
- Forced the USSR to compromise as he knew they could not afford to increase spending on arms.
- Had a strong relationship with Gorbachev.

The war in Afghanistan
- Criticised across the world. It cost billions and the lives of 15 000 Soviet troops.
- Gorbachev withdrew Soviet soldiers from the region in 1989 and this defeat made the USSR look weak.
- The huge expense of the war was very damaging for the Soviet economy.

Retrieval

Learn the answers to the questions below, then cover the answers column with a piece of paper and write as many as you can. Check and repeat.

Questions | Answers

#	Question	Answer
1	Which of Gorbachev's policies was named after the song 'My Way'?	The Sinatra Doctrine
2	Name the trade union formed in Poland led by Lech Wałęsa.	Solidarity
3	When were free elections held in Poland and what was the outcome?	June 1989; the communists lost and communism in Poland ended in August 1989
4	When did Berlin Wall come down?	November 1989
5	Who was the East German communist leader in 1989?	Honecker
6	Which communist leader in Romania brutally suppressed protests there in 1989?	Ceaușescu
7	How many different republics made up the USSR?	15
8	What happened on 1 July 1991?	The Warsaw Pact was officially dissolved
9	What month and year did politicians and members of the KGB attempt a coup in Russia?	August 1991
10	Name the Russian mayor who opposed the coup to remove Gorbachev from power in 1991.	Yeltsin
11	Who was left as the world's only superpower by the end of 1991?	The USA

Previous questions

Use the questions below to check your knowledge from previous chapters.

Questions | Answers

#	Question	Answer
1	Who replaced Antonín Novotný as leader of Czechoslovakia in 1968?	Dubček
2	How did the USSR end the Prague Spring?	By sending tanks into Prague in August 1968
3	What did the USA and the USSR agree at SALT II?	To limit delivery and placement of nuclear weapons / to ban ICBMs / to restrict use of missile launchers and bomber aircraft

8 The collapse of the USSR

Practice 8

Exam-style questions

1. **a)** Explain **one** consequence of Détente between the USA and the USSR in the 1970s. **(4)**

   > **EXAM TIP**
   > Remember to include your own contextual knowledge to explain the consequence.

   b) Explain **one** consequence of the Soviet invasion of Afghanistan in 1979. **(4)**

2. Write a narrative account analysing the key events that led to the fall of the Berlin Wall in 1989. **(8)**

   > You **may** use the following in your answer:
   > - Hungarian–Austrian border
   > - Mikhail Gorbachev
   >
   > You **must** also use information of your own.

3. Explain **two** of the following:
   - The importance of Gorbachev's 'new thinking' about Eastern Europe for the end of the Cold War. **(8)**

   > **EXAM TIP**
   > Think about the language you use when you explain the importance of events. Think of them as though they were on a continuum. So, was the event you are writing about:
   > - Vital
   > - Very important
   > - Quite important
   > - Important
   > - Not that important?

   - The importance of the opening of the border between East and West Germany for the end of the Cold War. **(8)**

   - The importance of the dissolution of the Warsaw Pact for the end of the Cold War. **(8)**

Great Clarendon Street, Oxford, OX2 6DP, United Kingdom

Oxford University Press is a department of the University of Oxford. It furthers the University's objective of excellence in research, scholarship, and education by publishing worldwide. Oxford is a registered trade mark of Oxford University Press in the UK and in certain other countries.

© Oxford University Press 2023

Written by Richard McFahn

Series Editor: Aaron Wilkes

The publisher would like to thank Kat O'Connor and Tim Williams for their work on the first edition of Edexcel GCSE History (9-1): Superpower relations and the Cold War 1941-91 Student Book (978-1382029858) on which this revision guide is based.

The moral rights of the author have been asserted

First published in 2023

All rights reserved. No part of this publication may be reproduced, stored in a retrieval system, or transmitted, in any form or by any means, without the prior permission in writing of Oxford University Press, or as expressly permitted by law, by licence or under terms agreed with the appropriate reprographics rights organization. Enquiries concerning reproduction outside the scope of the above should be sent to the Rights Department, Oxford University Press, at the address above.

You must not circulate this work in any other form and you must impose this same condition on any acquirer

British Library Cataloguing in Publication Data
Data available

9781382040433

10 9 8 7 6 5 4 3

The manufacturing process conforms to the environmental regulations of the country of origin.

Printed in the UK by Bell and Bain Ltd, Glasgow

Acknowledgements

The publisher would like to thank the following for permissions to use copyright material:

Photos: p8: Everett Collection Inc / Alamy Stock Photo; p14: Apic/Getty Images; p15: Everett Collection Historical / Alamy Stock Photo; p17: CBW / Alamy Stock Photo; p21: dpa picture alliance / Alamy Stock Photo; p28: CTK / Alamy Stock Photo; p32(tl): Utah/Shutterstock; p32(tr): octopusaga/Shutterstock; p32(b): mccool / Alamy Stock Photo; p34: Bill Waterson / Alamy Stock Photo; p35: Everett Collection Inc / Alamy Stock Photo; p39: Sueddeutsche Zeitung Photo / Alamy Stock Photo;

Artwork by Newgen, Aptara, Kamae Design, Moreno Chiacchiera, and Q2A Media

Although we have made every effort to trace and contact all copyright holders before publication this has not been possible in all cases. If notified, the publisher will rectify any errors or omissions at the earliest opportunity.

Links to third party websites are provided by Oxford in good faith and for information only. Oxford disclaims any responsibility for the materials contained in any third party website referenced in this work.

The manufacturer's authorised representative in the EU for product safety is Oxford University Press España S.A. of El Parque Empresarial San Fernando de Henares, Avenida de Castilla, 2 – 28830 Madrid (www.oup.es/en or product.safety@oup.com). OUP España S.A. also acts as importer into Spain of products made by the manufacturer.